TRAINING COUNSELL

Titles in the *Counsellor Trainer and Supervisor* Series

COUNSELLOR TRAINER AND SUPERVISOR SERIES

TRAINING COUNSELLORS

THE ASSESSMENT OF COMPETENCE

Sue Wheeler

CASSELL

London and New York

Cassell

Wellington House
125 Strand
London WC2R 0BB

127 West 24th Street
New York
NY 10011

British Library Cataloguing-in-Publication Data
A catalogue record for this book is available from the British Library.

First published 1996

ISBN 0–304–33348–4 (hardback)
0–304–33349–2 (paperback)

Typeset by York House Typographic Ltd, London
Printed and bound in Great Britain by Redwood Books, Trowbridge, Wiltshire

Contents

Acknowledgements

I was sitting quietly minding my own business in the Courses Recognition Group meeting in May 1994, when Windy Dryden passed me a note to ask whether I would like to write a book on the assessment of competence in counsellors. I passed it back without hesitation saying 'No thank you', but the seed was sown. I thought about it over the next few weeks and realized that I spent a lot of time thinking about assessment and counselling competence. I had asked for a term's study leave during the next year and decided to accept Windy's invitation and to combine writing the book with a relevant research project. I have appreciated Windy Dryden's encouragement and support and the time given by the School of Continuing Studies, the University of Birmingham. With the research I am most grateful to everyone who completed questionnaires, gave interviews or allowed me to use extracts from various documents they produced. Special thanks are due to the participants of the 1995 Madingley Conference for counsellor trainers in universities and to the Porch Room group. Carolyn Hicks, Fred Barwell and Ian Gallagher gave invaluable help with SPSS and statistical analysis.

I appreciate all the patient administrative help I have had, particularly from Pam Hobson but also from Carol Lawson, Sue Roston, Adrian Platts, Ivor Hayes and Rosemary Bolton. Sue Rose at BAC kindly gave her time to ensure that facts related to BAC matters were correct. John McLeod unselfishly gave me access to his resource bank on competence assessment both in discussion and with published and unpublished materials for which I am most grateful. Sue Izzard, my colleague and co-tutor on the counselling training course I am involved with, produced many of the assessment documents associated with our course and has been unerringly tolerant as I have shunted jobs her way to make time to write. As ever, Henry Miller gave advice, guidance, suggestions, time, attention, tea and sympathy at every stage of this writing process. Caroline Wheeler refined her editing skills, learned how to construct an index and cleaned the kitchen for months! Last but not least, a mention for Marvin, who kept my feet warm with his furry coat as I wrote until the end of his life in March 1995.

ONE

Introduction and overview

Counsellor training in Britain is a growth industry. Counselling courses exist in almost every town and city and new ones are created each year. While there exists a wide range of literature on an extensive range of counselling ideologies, theories and applications, texts that address aspects of counselling training are still relatively sparse. When designing a counselling training course, the trainer uses initiative and personal experience to produce a programme and associated assessment procedures, with or without reference to counselling training research evidence to inform their decisions.

Counselling is a relatively new profession in Britain, which has developed in a rather haphazard way. Professional standards have been painstakingly developed during the past decade by the British Association of Counselling (BAC) and benchmarks for counsellor competence have been set through the individual accreditation scheme (BAC, 1995a). Students can choose from courses that have different theoretical orientations, modes of delivery and methods of assessment with the knowledge that BAC accreditation, with its clearly defined criteria, is open to them provided they fulfill the requirements. Inclusion on the United Kingdom Register of Counsellors will follow from their individual accreditation.

The subject of this book is the assessment of competence of counsellors in training. It is written primarily for counselling trainers, to inform their course design and practice of assessment. It will also be of value to individual counsellors who are interested in evaluating their own competence when considering applying for individual accreditation with BAC. It provides a wealth of material for counselling trainers or counselling training researchers as they seek to design studies that will make a contribution to informing good practice in the counselling profession. The text brings together a summary of available research on counsellor competence and assessment and information about current practice including examples of assessment systems used in a range of organizations.

The term 'counselling' as used in this book needs to be defined. The word is widely used in its traditional sense of providing advice or guidance but here the meaning intended is more in line with the definition offered by BAC (1985, p.1), 'People become engaged in counselling when a person, occupying regularly or temporarily the role of counsellor, offers or agrees explicitly to offer time, attention and respect to another person or persons temporarily in the role of client'. A distinction is made between counselling as a discrete activity and the use of counselling skills, which are used as an adjunct to other skills in a role or job that is not exclusively about counselling.

There is considerable overlap between counselling as it is defined here and psychotherapy or therapy and sometimes the words are used inter-changeably. Psychotherapy is the term more often used when client work is concerned with inner experience rather than external events, when there is a focus on unconscious processes, when the therapeutic relationship is long-term and the client has an investment in resolving complex personal difficulties. Psychotherapy training is often organized differently to coun-selling training with more emphasis on personal therapy, training cases and supervision and less on the development of skills (Samuels, 1993). The main focus of this book will be on counselling training although mention will be made of psychotherapy particularly when making reference to research literature relevant to counselling training.

ORGANIZATIONS PROVIDING COUNSELLOR TRAINING

In 1995 the Directory of Counselling Training in Britain (BAC, 1995b) gave details of hundreds of courses in a range of institutions. The directory is not comprehensive as courses are not required to be included but it contains details of most current courses. Courses are run by large institu-tions such as universities and small private institutions operated by as few as one or two individuals. There are many courses organized by voluntary agencies such as Relate or the Westminster Pastoral Foundation. Some private organizations call themselves an institute, academy, college or foundation, while others have chosen a title such as 'Metanoia' or 'Routes' that conveys something of the flavour of their counselling. Little can be assumed about any of these organizations with respect to the type or quality of counselling training offered (Wheeler, 1994). A diploma course in one institution may offer a similar level of training as a certificate course in another. The quality and experience of staff in a small private agency may be superior to the staff of a course in a prestigious university.

The lack of homogeneity of institutions providing training is echoed in the type and level of counselling training offered. There are many models of counselling within the broad categories of humanistic, psychoanalytic and behavioural (Dryden *et al.*, 1989) counselling or psychotherapy. Courses range from short duration, brief introductions to counselling or counselling skills to diploma or masters' degree courses that provide an in-depth professional training. Some courses or combination of courses may fulfill the training requirement for BAC Accreditation. Counselling courses also exist for practitioners working with specific client groups, such as people with alcohol related problems, who are HIV +, those who have disabilities or individuals who have been bereaved, assaulted, raped or robbed. Courses for counsellors in general practice, in the workplace or in fertility treatment centres are some of the new developments in recent years. Some of these courses provide a comprehensive training for working with a particular client group or in a specific setting and others are aimed at experienced counsellors who have already completed a professional training but who wish to specialize.

ASSESSMENT AND GATEKEEPING

The diversity of counselling training opportunities described here sets the scene for the ensuing discussion about the assessment of competence. The level of assessment should be appropriate to the level of course taught, which in turn must provide clear information about the level of competence students can expect to achieve by the end of the course as well as the purpose for which their acquired competence can be used. Consider for example a counselling skills course for nurses. The course duration is thirty hours and its objective is to facilitate the development of listening, reflection and empathy skills that can be added to the nurses' repertoire of skills used in their routine nursing practice. The assessment of such a course would probably be designed to encourage the student to become a reflective practitioner (Schon, 1987), based on self observation and peer feedback. On the other hand if the course is set up to provide the necessary training to undertake more intensive counselling, the assessment criteria may need to be more stringent. The course tutor may use assessment to ensure that only those nurses who have grasped the basic principles of counselling and who are able to demonstrate fundamental skills, pass through the gate to a job more demanding of those skills.

This example introduces the notion of counselling competence assessment procedures fulfilling a gatekeeping function. Usually people who successfully complete counselling courses will use the qualification acquired to change or improve their employment prospects but some people take counselling courses out of general interest, to improve their quality of life or their relationships with other people. However this cannot be assumed when thinking about assessment, such people can choose not to be assessed and subsequently not be awarded a qualification. Both staff and students need to be clear about the level of course offered and the level or settings in which the knowledge and skill assimilated can be applied. The assessment process should ensure that students have achieved the required standard. For most of their working lives counsellors are alone with their clients in a room with minimal monitoring or evaluation of what takes place between them. It differs in the gravity of consequences from the responsibility afforded to airline pilots, who are alone (apart from the co-pilot) with their passengers miles away from trainer scrutiny once they have been granted their licence to practise. No one would advocate anything less than the most strict examination of a pilot and the licence to practise as a counsellor needs to be given with a similar sense of responsibility.

NATIONAL STANDARDS OF COUNSELLING COMPETENCE

Gradually national standards for assessing counselling competence are evolving through the efforts of BAC, the British Psychological Society (BPS), the United Kingdom Conference for Psychotherapy (UKCP) and the National Council for Vocational Qualifications (NCVQ).

BAC have developed the Individual Accreditation Scheme already mentioned, have been closely involved in the organization of the United Kingdom Register of Counsellors, introduced in 1996, and are responsible for the Counsellor Training Course Recognition Scheme. The Course Recognition Scheme has existed since 1988. A booklet (BAC, 1996) is produced that details criteria that courses need to meet in order to be eligible for recognition, which includes having a minimum of 400 taught hours. The criteria are flexible enough to encompass different counselling theories, modes of delivery, style of teaching, methods of assessment, etc. Courses can be helped to prepare for the recognition process by using a consultant who has experience of the scheme. If the course is considered to be appropriate for recognition, a panel is appointed by the course recognition group to scrutinize the application and arrange a visit to the course. Recognition is granted when the panel is satisfied that the training given is comprehensive and coherent with a core theoretical model and that the criteria for recognition are met. (See Chapter 8 for more information on national standards.) Students who have successfully completed a BAC recognized course are eligible for individual accreditation when they have logged a minimum of 450 hours of counselling practice. By this mechanism the Courses Recognition Scheme is linked to BAC individual accreditation.

The BPS have established a counselling psychology section and have sought to develop national standards for counselling psychologists. Part of the strategy has been the development of counselling psychology courses.

An outline structure has been agreed and organizations can apply to run such a course (Allen, 1990).

In 1993, the UKCP (United Kingdom Council for Psychotherapy) launched the first national register of psychotherapists. The UKCP accepts into membership organizations offering training or the validation of training. Therapists who have trained with or been approved by the organizations in membership are eligible for registration. This differs from the BAC Accreditation Scheme which approves individuals rather than organizations. The United Kingdom Register of Counsellors includes individuals with BAC Accreditation and organizations that train counsellors to work within them providing a counselling service. Counsellors registered through the organization that they work with are only registered to work within that agency. The assessment of competence is delegated to the registered agency, in common with the UKCP scheme.

In October 1992 the British Government stated their intention to support the development of National Vocational Qualifications which would (*Networks* 1994, p.4):

confirm and improve the position of the UK workforce by:

1) recognising its current skill level, and
2) providing a route for all to improve their skills and the quality of the service they provide.

The Lead Body for Advice, Guidance, Counselling and Psychotherapy was established. It includes representatives from many organizations including BAC, BPS and UKCP. The lead body have developed competency standards for counselling and counselling skills. Assessment of NVQs are criterion referenced, hence the competence of candidates is judged against pre-determined national performance standards. Competencies are grouped in units and units will be put together to create National Vocational Qualifications. A vast quantity of time and professional expertise has been invested in the development of NVQs. They will certainly provide the most comprehensive counselling assessment tools available although their reliabilty and effectiveness can only be tested when they are put into operation. These schemes will be described and discussed further in Chapter 8.

There are various examination boards that offer qualifications in counselling including the Royal Society of Arts (RSA), City and Guilds and the Associated Examining Board (AEB). While most universities offer their own validated qualifications some smaller organizations and private companies have chosen to prepare students for assessment through one of the examining boards in order to offer a recognizable qualification.

COUNSELLOR COMPETENCE AND THE CHALLENGE OF ASSESSMENT

Defining counsellor competence is no easy task. Competence has most regularly been evaluated in terms of skills, practical applications of counselling that can be isolated, observed and to some extent measured. Whether a person can be programmed to use a range of measurable skills and then perform effectively as a counsellor with a wide range of clients is doubtful. McLeod (1992) refers to 'competence' as 'any qualities or abilities of the person which contribute to effective performance of a role or task' (p.360) a broader description that takes account of the personal relationship (Rogers, 1957) or therapeutic alliance (Luborsky, 1976) that is an essential aspect of counselling. A framework for understanding the components of competence is required to assess whether trainee counsellors are developing appropriately and ultimately whether their counselling has reached a standard to warrant an award that gives them competent practitioner status.

The core components of counsellor competence have been suggested by various authors but vary in detail according to the theoretical model preferred. Crouch (1992) has offered a set of thirty-three competence statements under the general headings of counsellor awareness, personal work, theoretical understanding and casework skills. Connor (1994) describes a four-stage model of training that leads to competence moving through the stages of examining attitudes and values, acquiring knowledge and skills, the experience of client work and supervision and finally reflection and evaluation of counselling practice. McLeod (1993) has proposed six distinct components of competence, namely interpersonal skills, personal beliefs and attitudes, conceptual ability, personal 'soundness', mastery of technique and ability to understand and work within social systems. The BAC Course Recognition Scheme booklet (1996) specifies that trainee counsellors need to have an in-depth understanding of a core theoretical model of counselling and to have developed skills appropriate to that model. They should have opportunities for developing self awareness, be familiar with and adhere to codes of ethics, have experience with real clients under supervision and be aware of both the social issues that affect their work as counsellors and the relationship between counsellors and other mental health professionals.

Considering the diversity of components that contribute to competence it is inevitable that its assessment is a complex process that has to address varied factors. It seems unlikely that one form of assessment could provide a comprehensive and reliable measure. In practice a wide range of assessment techniques are used in counsellor training administered by course staff, students, external examiners/assessors, supervisors, managers and sometimes even clients.

The main body of this text will address the complexities of measuring and assessing competence. Chapter 2 discusses competence in detail and considers ways in which courses can organize training to help students achieve it. The third chapter focuses on the selection of students for counsellor training. While not part of a formative or summative assessment of competence it is during the selection stage that the crucial decision is made as to whether an applicant is suitable for counsellor training. Only those who are likely to be able to achieve the objectives set for a course in the time available and ultimately be successful in the final assessment should be accepted. The decision may relate to whether the selectors consider that the person will make a good counsellor or whether the candidate is likely to cope with the academic, emotional or financial demands of the course. Given the commitment in time, effort, emotional energy and money that counselling training entails the initial assessment of potential for ultimate success is of paramount importance.

Chapters 4 and 5 are linked and discuss ways and means of assessing competence, including the detail of what to assess and how to assess it. Chapter 4 suggests that all courses should be explicit about competencies that students should aspire to. Examples of competency statements devised by several courses with different theoretical orientations are given. This is followed by a discussion of all the people who could be involved in assessment, including course staff, students, clients, placement managers and external assessors.

Chapter 5 offers ideas and suggestions about methods of assessment. Counselling skills can be assessed in many different ways, using role play clients, real clients, video or audio tapes, case presentations, live counselling with observers, interactive video or computer programmes, written tests or in viva examinations. Feedback can be obtained from independent raters, supervisors, course staff, peers, clients or students can assess themselves. Assessors can use rating scales or intuition. The debate about NVQs centres around the issue of whether skills can or should be isolated from other aspects of competence. Skills are necessary but are they sufficient?

Self awareness is the topic of Chapter 6, an element of competence that is possibly the most important and probably the most difficult to assess. Traditional psychotherapy training schemes approach this problem head on by asking for a report from the trainee's analyst or therapist, commenting on whether they are ready to start their training in the first place and to complete their training when the time comes. If the analyst or therapist is not satisfied that the trainee has completed sufficient personal work then they are required to continue the therapy and delay completion of the course. Counselling training courses tend to shy away from making such demands on their trainees and personal therapy or group work experience is considered to be confidential. However some assessment has to be made about the trainee's ability to make a relationship with a client without judgement or prejudice or of their ability to facilitate the client's exploration of a wide range of issues without being handicapped by their own blind-spots.

Assessing personal development is one of the most contentious and demanding aspects of counsellor training and the activity which causes trainers to experience ethical conflicts and personal stress (McLeod, 1995). Chapter 7 draws on some of the author's own research into ethical dilemmas arising from the need to make judgements about competence when personal characteristics of trainees give cause for concern. The responsibility for being a gatekeeper of the counselling profession is considerable and failing a student at the end of a long and arduous training can be a painful experience for all concerned. Ideally it should never be allowed to happen given good selection procedures and continued support throughout the course but such events occur despite rigorous preventative measures being implemented.

The eighth chapter provides detailed information on the BAC individual accreditation scheme and on the assessment packages offered by public examination boards including NCVQ. The development of the NVQ competency-based assessment scheme for counsellors is traced and arguments for and against it are offered. It has already caused great controversy in the counselling profession and some of the implications are considered.

Quality assurance through external examiner participation in counsellor training, internal audit and the evaluation of training is the topic of Chapter 9. Assessment is an essential aspect of training but evaluation of the effectiveness of the training itself is also important. Research evidence attesting to the effectiveness of training initiatives is scant but suggestions are made about methods of evaluation. Finally attention is paid to complaints procedures, through which students and public can voice their discontent. Perhaps this is a sour note on which to end the book, but none the less an important topic to be covered to ensure that competence is fairly assessed.

TWO

What makes a good counsellor?

Before considering the assessment of competence in counsellors it is necessary to have a notion of what a good counsellor is. Many people can be good counsellors by providing help or support for their friends or colleagues through listening and showing concern but throughout this text counsellors referred to are those who seek to attain professional status and be eligible for employment to work with a broad range of clients. No assumptions can be made about universality of experience at the end of counsellor training. Unlike legal or medical training, which conform to national standards set by professional bodies, counsellor training is not regulated. Training courses are diverse, of varied length, depth and intensity. Some people offer their services as counsellors without having had any formal training and there is little to stop them. The individual BAC Accreditation scheme (1995) for instance includes provision for practitioners without formal training who have worked under supervision for a minimum of ten years to be eligible. Many professionals use counselling skills as part of their work and perform competently in their role, but 'only when both the user and the recipient explicitly agree to enter into a counselling relationship does it become "counselling" rather than the use of "counselling skills"' (BAC, 1990).

A professional counsellor is expected to be competent in working with a wide range of clients from diverse cultural backgrounds presenting a broad span of problems. The counselling task is to conceptualize the client's difficulties and to facilitate the process of development of self awareness and personal growth ultimately leading to the relief of symptoms or resolution of difficulties. The work must be conducted within an ethical framework that safeguards the interests of the client, which includes confidentiality, boundaries and limits to the personal involvement with the counsellor. The counsellor should make assessments of client difficulties and suggest appropriate treatment. 'It is an indication of the competence of counsellors when they recognise their inability to counsel a client or clients and make appropriate referrals' (BAC, 1990). They must monitor and evaluate their performance through clinical supervision. It is necessary for counsellors to conduct themselves in a professional manner, communicate clearly with others, establish a good working relationship with their clients and be consistent in their behaviour. They must manage their own stress, distinguish their own personal issues from those presented by the client and desist from counselling when their functioning is impaired due to personal or emotional difficulties, illness or other reason.

In this brief statement about the essential components of a professional counsellor comments have purposely been offered as generalizations to give a broad description that is true for counsellors using any counselling model. Crucial additions would have to be made to give a comprehensive account of a counsellor from a specific orientation, for example a client-centred counsellor would be described as having warmth and empathy, a psychodynamic counsellor, insight, and a behaviourist, the ability to design a treatment plan. It also describes the generalist counsellor who has not undergone specialist training to work with a specific client group.

Various authors have suggested ways of conceptualising a competent counsellor. For example McLeod (1993) suggests a composite model consisting of six distinct competence areas, which are (p.194):

1. *Interpersonal skills.* Competent counsellors are able to demonstrate appropriate listening, communicating, empathy, presence, awareness of non-verbal communication, sensitivity to voice quality, responsiveness to expressions of emotion, turn-taking, structuring of time, use of language.
2. *Personal beliefs and attitudes.* Capacity to accept others, belief in the potential for change, awareness of ethical and moral choices. Sensitivity to values helped by client and self.
3. *Conceptual ability.* Ability to understand and assess the client's problems, to anticipate future consequences of actions, to make sense of immediate process in terms of a wider conceptual scheme, to remember information about the client. Cognitive flexibility. Skill in problem solving.
4. *Personal 'soundness'.* Absence of personal needs or irrational beliefs which are destructive to counselling relationships, self confidence, capacity to tolerate strong or uncomfortable feelings in relation to clients, secure personal boundaries, ability to be a client. Absence of social prejudice, ethnocentrism and authoritarianism.
5. *Mastery of technique.* Knowledge of when and how to carry out specific interventions, ability to assess effectiveness of interventions, understanding of rationale behind techniques, possession of a sufficiently wide repertoire of interventions.

6. *Ability to understand and work within social systems.* Including awareness of the family and work relationship of the client, the impact of the agency on the client, the capacity to use support networks and supervision. Sensitivity to the social worlds of clients who may be from different gender, ethnic, sexual orientation or age group.

Connor (1995) has described a training model that leads to counsellor competence. The essential components of her model are:

Learning cycle stage 1: Attitudes and values

LEARNING OBJECTIVES

1. To become aware of personal assumptions and beliefs.
2. To explore and clarify values and attitudes.
3. To develop core therapeutic qualities.
4. To be aware of the ethical and professional issues and expectations in counselling.
5. To develop a personal code of professional ethics. (p.34)

Learning cycle stage 2: Knowledge and skills

LEARNING OBJECTIVES

1. To become familiar with major counselling theories and approaches.
2. To develop a thorough working knowledge of a core theoretical model.
3. To focus upon the therapeutic process in relation to change.
4. To understand the major causes and manifestations of client problems, including developmental psychology and an understanding of mental health and mental illness.
5. To understand family and social systems, organisations and contexts.
6. To appreciate the work of helping agencies.
7. To practise the counselling skills necessary for competence in the core theoretical model.
8. To learn, and to apply, a variety of helping strategies and interventions.
9. To identify and own personal strengths and limitations in relation to skills and strategies.
10. To develop an integrated counselling style. (p.42)

Learning cycle stage 3: Client work and supervision

LEARNING OBJECTIVES

1. To distinguish between counselling and other helping activities.
2. To set up counselling contracts with real clients.
3. To practise counselling competencies in real counselling situations.
4. To regularly reflect upon counselling practice through use of a counselling log, case notes and learning journal.
5. To experience regular supervision, both individual and group.
6. To develop the internal supervisor.
7. To develop confidence as a counsellor. (p.50)

Learning cycle stage 4: Reflection and evaluation

LEARNING OBJECTIVES

1. To reflect continuously upon learning both in the course and in work with real clients.
2. To engage in, and learn from, the process of assessment: self peer and tutor assessment.
3. To become familiar with research processes which are appropriate in the field of counselling.
4. To become actively engaged in counselling research. (p.53)

Models of competence developed by Overholzer (1993), Crouch (1992), and Combs (1986) are referred to in Chapters 4 and 5.

Another way of looking at counsellor competence has been devised by the author and is illustrated in Figure 2.1. It has five components described as follows:

1. SELF – *presentation, preservation and professionalism*

Presenting themselves to the client in an acceptable way. Containing own anxieties and having coping strategies for looking after self. Maintaining therapeutic boundaries and engaging in professional development.

2. OTHER – *centredness*

Being able to focus full attention on the client and process client material in a thoughtful and therapeutic way.

3. RELATIONSHIP

Establish a relationship that enables the work to take place. A climate of trust, understanding and confidence. Demonstrating respect and communicating empathy with client. Forging a therapeutic alliance.

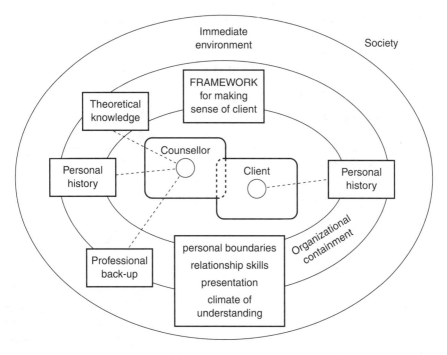

Figure 2.1 *The five components of counsellor competence*

4. THE THERAPEUTIC FRAME

Using theory and skills to conceptualize client material. Making assessments and contracting. Being sensitive to confidentiality and ethics.

5. ENVIRONMENT – *social, cultural, economic, geographic*

Awareness of the context of therapy. Other services available. Social, economic and cultural background of clients. Awareness of historical, organizational or geographical aspects of immediate environment.

1. SELF – PRESENTATION, PRESERVATION AND PROFESSIONALISM

Counsellors must present themselves to clients in such a way that they inspire confidence that they have the potential to be helpful. Presentation may include dress and physical aspects of appearance but is also concerned with interpersonal communication style. A rough and aggressive manner would be unlikely to set the tone for intimate conversation, regardless of theoretical competence. Various studies have linked aspects of presentation to subsequent client improvement. Strong (1968) suggested that in the first instance the therapist establishes themselves as attractive, trustworthy and expert which gives them the 'persuasive' power to establish the necessary conditions for therapeutic change to happen. Grimes and Murdock (1989) and LaCrosse (1980) also studied attractiveness, trustworthiness and expertness as perceived by clients in the initial interview and found them to be related positively to symptom change and client commitment to therapy, measured in terms of attendance rates. Heppner and Claiborn (1989) found that non-verbal behaviours such as smiling have a greater effect on the client's perception of their competence as therapists than verbal behaviour or therapy content. McConnaughy (1987) maintains that it is the 'personal development, interpersonal style and life experiences of the therapist that shape the emotional climate, theoretical perspective and techniques that the therapist offers to clients' (p.303).

The term self preservation covers many issues. Counselling is a vocation or job, an activity that produces personal satisfaction and/or financial reward and needs to be contained as separate from other aspects of the counsellor's life. At the end of sessions counsellors need to be able to leave their clients' concerns behind. They should be able to distinguish clearly between their own psychopathology and that of their clients, in order to use the counselling relationship appropriately. Counselling can be stressful and demanding (Brady *et al.*, 1995) and support systems and coping strategies are essential to ensure that they are emotionally as well as physically available for therapeutic practice.

Professionalism covers diverse aspects of a counsellor's practice, ranging from the ability to communicate with mental or other health professionals to keeping accurate accounts and adherence to codes of ethics. It includes a commitment to continual professional development through supervision, training and self reflection, as well as monitoring and evaluation of their own professional conduct and competence. A critical awareness of personal limitations is essential to ensure that clients are referred to other agencies when appropriate.

2. OTHER-CENTREDNESS

Self awareness is essential for the counsellor but they must also be able to focus attention on their client. Inherent in this ability is a natural curiosity, interest and concern for others. Rogers (1951) has written extensively on the need to be non-judgemental and to regard the client positively. This is not as simple as it sounds, for example when faced with someone who has committed heinous crimes or who has offensive racist or sexist beliefs. The task of the counsellor is to engage with the whole person with optimism about the potential for change although with due regard to the notion that the client may not wish to make the changes that the counsellor would see as desirable. Setting aside one's own value system and entering into the realm of another's attitudes, beliefs and values requires great skill as well as self containment. The agenda for counselling belongs to the client, which is regularly a source of frustration for the therapist, particularly when issues that seem of paramount importance are avoided. The counsellor must tolerate the client making what they perceive to be mistakes or foolish decisions, usually without direct intervention, recognizing the client's autonomy. Sometimes, having conceptualized the client's problem from their presentation, history, value system and cultural background, within a theoretical model, the decision has to be made that counselling will not help. This is an important aspect of being 'other' focused, an assessment of the client's needs and motivation must be made and appropriate recommendations made.

When considering being 'other' focused, the counsellor should be trained to face any issues that clients may present. They may be called upon to work with clients who present depression, anxiety or loneliness, who are troubled by their sexuality, illness or disability or who have been bereaved or traumatized by abuse, accident, war or natural disaster. The counsellor must be able to tolerate strong feelings of despair, rage or even the client's erotic feelings toward them and make sense of them within whichever theoretical model they have studied.

3. RELATIONSHIP

Although models of counselling vary in their interpretation of the counselling relationship and its purpose in the process of therapy, all would agree that a good working relationship is essential. A consistent predictor of positive outcome in counselling and therapy has been the therapeutic alliance (Luborsky, 1976), that encompasses the real relationship that develops between counsellor and client. The alliance includes trust, respect, understanding, empathy and co-operation in the therapeutic process. Understanding of the therapeutic alliance has developed from the work on core conditions carried out by Rogers (1957). He postulated that for personal change to occur as part of a therapeutic relationship the following conditions should be met:

- the therapist should be genuine in relation to the client, being aware of his/her own feelings and not hiding them from the client
- the therapist should regard the client positively, as someone of unconditional self worth, of value regardless of his/her behaviour or feelings
- the therapist responds to the client with empathy, attempting to understand his/her communication by adopting the client's internal frame of reference

Rogers described these conditions as necessary and sufficient but while many counselling theoreticians would agree that the conditions are necessary, few would describe them as sufficient. McLeod (1994) discusses the contributions of Jerome Frank (1973), who argued that therapy is effective because of non-specific factors such as a supportive relationship rather than therapeutic strategies and techniques. Grencavage and Norcross (1990) surveyed therapists and reported that the highest level of consensus between them related to the importance of the therapeutic alliance (56 per cent cited this factor). In a review of reviews Patterson (1984) concludes that there are few things in the field of psychology for which the evidence is so strong as the necessity for accurate empathy, respect or warmth and therapeutic genuineness in counselling relationships. Lietaer (1992) studied the helpful or hindering processes in client centred therapy and found that clients most frequently referred to the relationship aspect of sessions as having an impact on immediate outcome. The most helpful therapy hour is reported by clients as being one in which they 'have as much space as possible to work out a solution to his or her problem in the context of an emotionally secure relationship' (Llewelyn *et al.*, 1987).

4. THE THERAPEUTIC FRAME

The therapeutic frame includes the space in which the counselling takes place, the theoretical model and techniques that inform practice and the code of ethics that protects clients. The counselling room must be organized to facilitate the development of a therapeutic alliance, hence, safe, consistent, comfortable and confidential in a building that is accessible, and within an organization that is sympathetic to the aims of counselling. The theoretical frame is the knowledge and understanding that the counsellor uses to inform their practice, which will vary greatly between theoretical orientations. The skills and interventions used to facilitate the counselling process are derived from that theoretical frame. The conceptual frame is the synthesis between theoretical knowledge and material presented by the client that underpins the counselling strategy. Finally the ethical frame refers to the code of ethics to which the counsellor adheres to define boundaries and personal conduct.

This broad title of the therapeutic frame covers many crucial aspects of counselling. In her thought-provoking paper on managing the frame in general practice, Hoag (1992) highlights the importance of managing the detail involved in counselling practice, including the need to have a shared understanding of the nature of the counselling relationship with all who work in the practice, to have control of the appointments, to have a system for referrals and to be able to see clients regularly in the same room.

In recent years both the importance and the complexity of counselling ethics have been afforded considerable attention. Ethical codes may seem straightforward until they are challenged and the situations that are marginal cause the most soul searching. Bond (1993) has provided an excellent tome on the complexities of counselling ethics that both states legal and ethical positions on a wide range of topics, including confidentiality, disclosure of child sexual abuse and financial management, and also offers guidance in negotiating tortuous situations.

The theoretical frame in which counselling takes place is both vital and controversial. There are numerous counselling theories derived from psychoanalytic, humanistic and behavioural traditions, most of which can be broadly described as integrative as all models draw on the wealth of literature on therapeutic practice. The theoretical model of counselling must relate to a model of human growth and development and have congruent skills and techniques. However there is considerable disagreement about which bits of different theories can be integrated (Wheeler, 1992). While eclecticism is in many respects laudable if a counsellor is truly well trained in several different models and can choose to work in one or other model as appropriate to the problem presented by the client, there is a danger that theoretical models can be merged in an unclear way that leaves the counsellor floundering and the client confused. Some courses require students to study two models in depth and the Course Recognition Criteria developed by BAC (1996) dictate that students should have a consistent training in one core theoretical model (which may be integrative or to some extent eclectic) as well as an introduction to a contrasting model or models.

Finally the frame refers to the interaction in the counselling encounter, the stance taken by the counsellor and the interventions made. This includes the nature of the relationship, skills and techniques employed to facilitate change. When considering competencies and assessment it is often this aspect of the counsellor's work that receives most attention. Counsellor behaviour in the room is observable by various means and to some extent measurable. Verbal interventions provide a window on the theoretical stance taken and the self awareness of the counsellor. Verbal responses can be analysed and skills identified using methods devised by Carkhuff (1969).

5. ENVIRONMENT – SOCIAL, CULTURAL, ECONOMIC, GEOGRAPHIC

Counselling does not take place in a vacuum, independent of its environment. The client, counsellor and the organization within which they meet are inextricable from the society of which they are a part. The influence of the external world needs to be taken into account alongside the pressures that result from intra-psychic processes. Social and political changes affect people in both dramatic and subtle ways that are not always immediately obvious, particularly if they are outside the counsellor's own experience. For example a man suffering from stress at work may be helped when he recognizes that his environment has changed. His expectation of a job for life and his personal value of giving loyalty and commitment to the company are challenged by the notion of portable skills, a mobile workforce and a 'hire and fire' management culture. He is still personally challenged by his new circumstances but can begin to re-assess and adjust when he faces the problem created by a shift in the value system of the organization.

The main focus of counsellor training tends to be on work with individuals. Problems presented are seen as located within the individual who is empowered through the counselling process to make changes, adjust or accommodate their circumstances. Woolfe (1983) argues that counsellors need to be made more aware of how to empower their clients to share their concerns with others with similar problems and organize themselves to challenge authorities that have the power to change policies or to provide resources that can have an impact on their lives. In other words that clients who are the victims of their environment should be helped to become more political. This could apply to various groups who feel oppressed by their environment, the unemployed, single parents, ethnic minorities, gays or lesbians and those who are disadvantaged in other ways.

Cultural considerations are important to all counsellors. Assumptions about class or ethnic cultural background, values or beliefs must be made with care because of the risk of stereotyping. Western culture tends to be individualistic, in which responsibility lies with individuals, whereas some cultures regard responsibility as more collective. Not all women of South Asian origin have arranged marriages but sometimes those that do are unhappy about it. Should there be an expectation that she could respond to her circumstances in the same way as a white woman might? Encouraging an individual solution to the problem may alienate the client from their family or community and this may or may not be seen as a preferred solution. The whole family may have to be involved in decision making, with or without the help of the counsellor.

The counsellor must attempt to take account of the social, economic and cultural situation of the client or clients. However, it is as well to recognize that the counsellor's own situation and the process of counselling is itself located within a middle-class social position. Further, the practice of counselling with its reliance on the symbolic use of language, particularly with respect to culture and class, may limit the accessibility, acceptability, appropriateness or utility of much counselling practice to wide sections of the population. This needs careful contemplation.

The organization in which the counsellor works also impacts on them and their clients. It will influence the way in which counselling is perceived, how it is offered, to whom it is offered, facilities available, number of sessions for clients allowed, as well as stability of the service and job security for the counsellor. It may provide a secure environment for the work to take place, or one that is obstructive and hence stressful for all involved. The counsellor's energy may concentrate on the counselling or on trying to influence the organization.

COMPETENCE

Considering these dimensions of a good counsellor, questions about competence follow. What is a competent counsellor? What is the pathway to achieving competence? How can competence be assessed? But first the meaning of competence must be explored.

Schon (1987) defines competence as enlightened action involving a complex mix of skill and judgement in which critical capacities are all important. In recent years there has been considerable pressure from government sources to define and measure competence in many vocational arenas including counselling. The Lead Body for Advice, Guidance, Counselling and Psychotherapy has been working for several years to produce relevant competencies and associated performance criteria for counsellors (see Chapter 8). There is some scepticism about the efficacy about reducing counselling to a list of competencies, albeit a long list, and particularly about the impact on counsellor development that a competency-based scheme may have. While the development of skills, both generic and pertinent to a specific counselling orientation is widely acknowledged as a necessary part of counsellor training it is not considered to be sufficient. In writing about training in psychodynamic therapy, Strupp *et al.* (1988) reviews training programmes that teach specific techniques broken down into observable components and says, 'although such programs do change behaviour of very inexperienced trainees, we question the wisdom of teaching therapeutic skills that are not anchored by a broader conception of professional development' (p.690).

Barnett (1994) has suggested four criteria for the application of the term skill that are relevant to counselling. Skills involve:

1. A situation of some complexity.
2. A performance that addresses the situation, is deliberate and is not just a matter of chance.
3. An assessment that the performance has met the demands of the situation.
4. A sense that the performance was commendable.
    (p.56)

He draws the distinction between skills that require a high degree of cognitive insight (e.g. as performed by a surgeon) and those that require less (e.g. driving a car) and suggests that in some situations in order to be skilful and perform effectively a sophisticated knowledge base is needed to inform the choice of skills to be applied. With respect to counselling the capacity to assess and conceptualize the difficulties of any client who presents themselves could be defined in terms of a set of skills that depend on an extensive body of knowledge and experience. Achieving competence in applying such skills will be the result of considerable experience probably guided by a more experienced practitioner, namely a supervisor.

Supervision of clinical practice is essential to the development and maintenance of clinical competence but Shaw and Dobson (1988) observed that the effectiveness of supervision for producing therapist competency can only be assessed when necessary skills and criteria for professional competence of therapists have been defined.

How specific competencies can be filtered from a model of what makes a good counsellor is a challenge that has been taken up not only by the Lead Body for Advice, Guidance, Counselling and Psychotherapy development team but also by individuals and training course leaders. Several examples of competence statements are reproduced in Chapter 4.

Given the author's model of a good counsellor, competence overall would need to reflect competence in each domain. It is easier to talk about competence in describing the management of the therapeutic frame than it is with respect to self awareness or the environment. 'Competently self aware' is a phrase that is unlikely to be used in describing a counsellor or trainee although the course tutors will usually have some notion of adequate self awareness. Evidence of the development of self awareness is a regular requirement in counsellor training (see Chapter 6). One component of that self awareness would undoubtedly be the ability to recognize personal limitations of competence and to deal with them appropriately.

Similarly, environmental competence is not easy to define but specific competencies have been developed related to cross cultural counselling (Sodowsky *et al.*, 1994). However it is possible to assemble evidence drawn from many sources including counselling practice, supervision, group work, seminar presentation, tutorials and informal observations that would demonstrate social, political and cultural consciousness or lack of it.

Competence in the domains, described as 'other', therapeutic frame and relationship can be defined, demonstrated and evaluated by various means. The ability to focus intently on the world of the 'other' or client is essential to any counselling relationship. That capability can be observed not only through the evaluation of real or role play counselling but also in more informal settings. In any social gathering some people demonstrate an ability to listen to others without interrupting while others tend to dominate conversations and not take their turn. The ability to develop and maintain a counselling relationship can be observed and even measured if necessary using therapeutic alliance scales (Marmar *et al.*, 1989).

Competence in maintaining the therapeutic frame is multi-faceted. It involves the assimilation of a body of knowledge that can be readily tapped and used during the counselling interview. Robinson (1974) has described the stages of the development of competence as:

1. unconscious incompetence
2. conscious incompetence
3. conscious competence
4. unconscious competence

which are highly relevant to counselling as theoretical knowledge is most helpful when it unconsciously informs action. By the end of a counselling training course, students will usually be consciously competent in most areas which will become unconscious competence given time and experience. Skills competence is probably the most straightforward to define and measure although caution is urged that such competence is not taken out of context of the therapeutic frame as a whole. Sexton and Whiston (1991) refer to the counselling process being dependent on the counsellor client relationship which underpins all that happens in a session including the use of specific techniques or interventions supporting the argument that skills competence alone is meaningless. Martin (1990) also argues that psychological skills training must be integrated into a more comprehensive educational experience. Competence in using the therapeutic frame includes the ability to use a range of skills that adhere to the core theoretical model used in practice. The development and use of therapy manuals particularly for use in research, provide comprehensive documentation of how a therapeutic intervention should be conducted, against which skills and other competencies can be evaluated (Strupp et al., 1988).

In summary a competent counsellor is one who is worldly wise, self aware, well informed theoretically, who has skills congruent with the theoretical model used and can make a good therapeutic alliance. The competent counsellor can make assessments of clients and decide appropriately who they can and cannot work with, what to do and what not to do. The counsellor must be able to communicate with other professionals and make appropriate referrals. Ultimately a competent counsellor is someone who can manage their own stress and take care of themselves so that they are able to give full attention to the client. Put more simply in Carkhuff's terms (1969), counsellors must be just a little bit ahead of their clients.

TRAINING ELEMENTS

The need to develop competence across the broad spectrum described in the competence model proposed by the author has implications for the elements of training that are essential to a good course, which will in turn have implications for methods of assessment. Training is discussed here as it relates to the five dimensions of the model.

1. Self – presentation, preservation and professionalism

For counsellors to be confident, able to look after themselves and professional in their performance the first concern will be to select people who seem suitable and who are likely to fulfil the requirements of the course. Selection is discussed in detail in Chapter 3. Personal development will inevitably play a major part in all training courses, facilitated by a range of means, including experiential groupwork, personal therapy, residential training, tutorials, personal development groups and personal/professional journals. Some aspects of professionalism will probably be addressed through lectures, tutorials and seminars both experientially and with reference to relevant literature.

The impact of personal therapy on trainee counsellors has been the topic of considerable debate (see Clark, 1986; Macaskill, 1988; Macaskill, 1992; Wheeler, 1991). Trainee counsellors have the opportunity to address their own personal problems or deal with stressful life events but some courses are reluctant to make therapy compulsory. Even when personal therapy is a course requirement there is no guarantee that it will be used productively, but many students choose to find a therapist at some point during their training. It could be regarded as a preventative measure to deal with stress and burn out (Norcross and Prochaska, 1986). However reviews of the impact of personal therapy on counsellor performance have only occasionally produced a positive association (Buckley *et al.*, 1981) and have more often revealed an insignificant or negative relationship between the two variables (Wheeler, 1991; Macaskill, 1992).

Sometimes counselling training courses include a personal development group as a vehicle for enhancing self awareness and self esteem. Students often report that they have benefited from such a group (Small and Manthei, 1988; Izzard and Wheeler, 1994) and some studies have found that attitudes, values, self esteem and awareness have changed or increased as a result of the group experience (O'Leary *et al.*, 1994; Page and O'Leary, 1992).

Training that involves a residential component is often included in courses. When a group stays together for several days, group tensions and interpersonal behaviour tend to be highlighted in a more intense way than during weekly meetings. Given space and support to address some of the interpersonal issues that are raised, personal learning can be considerable. Goldie (1995) describes an outdoor experience weekend organized as part of a counselling training course designed to enhance self awareness. Although students were extremely anxious in anticipation of the event, most both

enjoyed the weekend and reported gaining insight into aspects of themselves and others they had previously been unaware of.

2. Other-centredness

Learning to be 'other' centred can be achieved in several ways, through the
development of self awareness, through life experience and exposure to
diverse populations, by studying theories of human growth and development, and through the enhancement of skills of attending to verbal and non-
verbal behaviour. The ability to listen has often been described as the
therapist's major asset.

Selection of counsellors for training will be important in this dimension.
People often seek counselling training when they primarily need therapy for
themselves and seek to repair their own psyche through intimate interaction
with others (Henry *et al.*, 1971; Guy, 1987). Individuals who have a capacity
for self-abnegation (Guy, 1987) and who are able to set aside their own
needs including the temptation to talk about themselves in the therapy hour
will make better counsellors. Therapists' own psychic wounds are not
necessarily a negative indicator of their ability to help others, as personal
experience can be very valuable but selection for training must take account
of their degree of disturbance, awareness of difficulties and of steps taken to
process their experience in the wake of trauma (Goldberg, 1988).

Awareness of others and their difficulties can be heightened through
various forms of experiential learning. For example, simple exercises such
as being led around blindfolded or trying to negotiate a building in a
wheelchair can give unique insight into the everyday experience of a
disabled person. Racism awareness training is usually experiential and
exercises are designed to give individuals a taste of what it is like to be part
of a minority. A powerful exercise used in sexual abuse training involves
being asked to tell someone else a closely guarded personal secret, which
usually leads to a better understanding of the terror that goes with the
disclosure of abuse.

Listening skills, essential to a good counsellor, are taught and practised in
the early stages of counselling training, but may be the subject of developmental work throughout several years of a course. The development and
maintenance of 'other' awareness will evolve through role play with other
students and later through clinical work with clients under supervision.
Supervision focuses attention on the 'other', the client, as well as their
relationship with the counsellor. Counsellors' concerns should be taken to
their own therapist, thus separating their needs from those of the client. In
the early days of a supervisory relationship with a trainee, skills training is
most important (Stoltenberg and Delworth, 1987), but the emphasis shifts
as confidence and competence develops.

3. Relationship

Training work on the therapeutic relationship is conducted primarily through skills training. Continued work on self awareness will contribute to the development of better therapeutic relationships as the counsellor becomes more at ease with themselves and hence with others. The importance of the therapeutic relationship will be reinforced through reference to the therapeutic alliance. Supervision also contributes to awareness of relationship issues, although each model of counselling has its own definition of how the relationship should be used. For example in psychodynamic or person centred practice, the major focus of supervision would be the therapeutic relationship, whereas in cognitive therapy it would be considered less important. Personal qualities of the counsellor will affect the counselling relationship hence once again, the ability to establish a supportive counselling relationship will feature highly amongst selection criteria.

Role play triad exercises (with a counsellor, client and observer), with or without a video camera, provide good opportunities for learning skills and observing the counselling relationship. The observer can make notes and give feedback on the interaction between the counsellor and client or a group, including the tutor, can watch and comment on the video recording.

4. The therapeutic frame

Counselling students will spend much of their time engaged in learning about theory, relating it to practice and practising skills. Activities involved will include substantial amounts of reading, attending lectures and seminars, presenting topics or case studies, skills practice using role play, audio or video recording, writing essays, writing up case notes, counselling real clients on placement and clinical supervision.

There is very little research evidence for the most effective ways of training counsellors and sometimes opportunities for gaining greater insight have been missed. For instance Moncher and Prinz (1991) reviewed 359 treatment outcome studies and concluded that most ignored or failed to adequately assess therapist competence or skills as a variable in treatment efficacy. A review of the research on counselling training (Ford, 1979) revealed scant evidence that training interventions enhanced students' performance sufficiently to ensure that clients benefited. Alberts and Edelstein (1990) found that there was some support for instruction, modelling and feedback as training methods for enhancing interview skills. There are currently no training studies that focus on complex integration, application and evaluation of skills on a theoretical and empirical basis (Bergin and Garfield, 1994).

Microskills training is widely used on counsellor training courses (Ivey, 1971). The micro-training model has been applied to major theoretical models and has defined and isolated techniques, interventions, skills and postures applicable to each model that can be taught systematically through role play and video experiences. Counselling skills can be taught in many different ways, the use of counsellor, client and observer triads, time out techniques and variants of the fish-bowl exercise (Jacobs, 1992) being particularly popular.

As in psychotherapy training (Samuels, 1993) there is considerable reliance on supervision of clinical practice to facilitate the development of skills and other facets of the frame. Like the debate about personal therapy, supervision is considered to be essential to counselling practice both during training and throughout a counselling career, although there is little empirical evidence of the effectiveness of supervision. It has been observed (Wiley and Ray, 1986) that supervised trainees increase their ability to understand their impact on clients and to incorporate a theoretical framework for their work, but there was no evidence that specific therapy skills resulted from supervision.

It would be an essential part of any training course to include lectures, seminars or other forms of teaching about Codes of Ethics. At first sight the BAC Code of Ethics seems quite straightforward, something that could be taken away, read and forgotten. Upon closer scrutiny it is not difficult to find topics that produce furious debate on ethical grounds. Confidentiality for example may seem quite straightforward until a case is cited that challenges assumptions and values. If a client leaves a counselling session determined to commit suicide, what if anything, does the counsellor do? When a long-standing client discloses fantasies about his thirteen-year-old daughter and the counsellor suspects that they are not just fantasies, how do they respond? Counselling ethics have been discussed in great detail by Bond (1993) and all courses will need to give students the opportunity to absorb some of the many ethical complexities.

5. Environment – social, cultural, economic, geographic

It is doubtful that 'environment training' would ever be seen on a course syllabus, but most courses will include sessions that cover relevant topics. These might include racism awareness sessions and cross cultural counselling training. Class, disability, gender and sexual orientation awareness should have a place. The social context of counselling, might be the topic of one or more sociology seminars. Organizational dynamics and group behaviour will be a feature of any good course. The composition of the course group will make a substantial contribution to environment awareness if it is chosen to represent all aspects of a community. This is not always easily achieved as counselling training tends to attract more women than men and few candidates from ethnic minorities. Nevertheless attention paid to recruitment procedures or the provision of bursaries can encourage a wider range of students.

Assignments can be set to encourage students to think about counselling in a social, political or cultural context. Trainers and lecturers can pay attention to cultural, organizational or political dimensions to any topic they present. They may need to continually remind themselves that counselling individuals is only one way of facilitating change and that sometimes activities that involve confronting the environmental source of problems experienced by individuals are a better focus of energy and give clients more power.

SUMMARY

This chapter has considered factors that contribute towards a person being a good counsellor. It has described a broad model of counsellor competence and suggested some ways in which the development of competence can be achieved through counsellor training. There has been an emphasis on the qualities that a person needs to become a good counsellor, expanded further in the next chapter, which addresses issues related to the selection of counsellor trainees.

THREE

Selection of trainees: the most crucial phase of assessment

Counselling is an attractive profession for many people for numerous reasons. It is perceived to be a job for which candidates see themselves as having relevant skills. Such people describe themselves as being good listeners, having a keen interest in people, wanting to help others, and being someone to whom others gravitate towards to share their problems. They have sometimes had some form of counselling themselves which they have found helpful or have survived some major personal tragedy, illness or life event that has inspired them to try and help others get through similar life crises. They have often had a vocational training in one of the 'caring' professions and feel frustrated by the limitations imposed on them by the nature of their employment. Counselling trainers are faced with the complex task of selecting from such hopeful applicants, those who seem to be the most likely to be successful in achieving the level of competence as counsellors that the course will expect at its conclusion. The selection process is probably the most crucial assessment procedure for any course, whether it takes place at the beginning of training, or at some point during the course, typically after a first introductory year. 'In a very real way, admission into an advanced training program in psychotherapy is the first gate or 'rite of passage' in the journey to becoming a psychotherapist' (Guy, 1987, p.34). Mistakes made at the selection stage can cause considerable grief for trainers. Students who struggle with the course or whose personal characteristics make their performance as counsellors questionable are highly demanding on staff time. There is need for clarity on the part of the selectors about what they are looking for, and a set of criteria to help with the choice.

This chapter reviews some of the literature on selection for counselling training both in terms of suitability and selection processes. It also draws on original research undertaken by the author through a survey of British counselling training courses, through interviews with course organizers and participation in a seminar on selection attended by eminent university counselling course trainers at a conference in Cambridge in 1995.

WHAT DO WE KNOW ABOUT WHO IS SUITABLE FOR COUNSELLING TRAINING?

In terms of empirical research there has been little success in defining the ideal personality traits, personal qualities, attitudes, or life experiences that correlate with counselling competence and positive outcome for clients. Much of the information available is phenomenological, derived from observation and personal experience but none the less affords us some insight into positive and negative characteristics. While counselling and psychotherapy training is sometimes different, the nature of the work has many similarities. A relationship has to develop between therapist and client, boundaries must be respected and the therapist needs to be aware of and manage their own psychological problems. Hence, given the dearth of literature on personal suitability for counsellor training, reference is made to research relating to the selection of psychotherapists, clinical psychologists and even psychiatrists.

In his work, *The Personal Life of the Psychotherapist* Guy (1987) lists some of the aspects of a person that make them either suitable or unsuitable to be a psychotherapist. He lists functional qualities as being: curious and inquisitive, the ability to listen comfortably in conversation, emotionally insightful, introspective, capable of self denial, tolerant of ambiguity, capable of warmth and caring, tolerant of intimacy, comfortable with power, able to laugh. His disfunctional qualities include: too much emotional distress, vicarious coping methods, loneliness and isolation, desire for power and vicarious rebellion. Although Guy lists capability for self denial amongst functional qualities, caution is urged in how this is interpreted. Counselling in Britain has a long history founded in voluntary work for which the capacity for self denial has been paramount. In examining the personal values of counsellors and comparing them with outcome for clients (Lafferrty *et al.*, 1989), some evidence was found that the more effective counsellors placed significantly less importance on having comfortable and exciting lives. However the importance of counsellors taking care of themselves, materially, physically and emotionally should not be underestimated (Syme, 1995).

Selectors for counselling training may be looking for particular qualities that would be compatible with the course's theoretical orientation, as well as looking for candidates who show an active interest and understanding of the model offered. For example Strupp *et al.* (1988) looked at literature relating to the selection of candidates for psychoanalytic therapy training and quoted the Holt and Luborsky (1958) study of participants in psychiatric training. They found various characteristics that correlated with supervisors' evaluations of overall competence. These included genuineness rather than artificiality, social adjustment with co-workers, freedom from status mindedness, self objectivity, mature heterosexual adjustment and adequate emotional control. Combs (1986) was interested in what makes a good helper using a person centred approach. He found indications that being an effective helper related to the perceptual organization and personal beliefs of the helper with respect to empathy, self, what people are like and sense of purpose.

While counselling trainers may have in mind the model of counselling they adhere to, when selecting potential students, McConnaughy (1987) argues that it is character and interpersonal style that determine the nature of the therapy offered to clients, the mix of theoretical model and unique personal qualities through chemical reaction will produce a unique counselling style. However he asserts that in all cases the therapist must be capable of intimacy with the client.

McLeod (1995) explores the notion that there are generic competencies, that can be enhanced through training that potential counsellors must have in order to achieve professional competence. Such generic competencies must include some basic skills such as the ability to listen and respond appropriately to communication from others and attitudes and beliefs that are benevolent, but the ultimate taxonomy of such competencies is yet to be determined and he suggests it should be an urgent focus of future research. Safinofsky (1979) said something similar: 'He [the potential counsellor] must already be a concerned, compassionate, intelligent and sensitive human being before his training even begins. Training may mature and refine the experience of his concern and empathy but it cannot supply what does not exist in the first place' (p.195).

Various other observations have been made about skills or attributes of therapists that are associated with ultimate competence that may be discernible by various means at the selection stage. Shaw and Dobson (1988) have suggested that clinical memory, the ability to take in and hold on to details of the client's history, is associated with positive outcome. The ability to conceptualize client material is a skill that can be refined and developed but may be a generic competence (Kivlighan and Quigley, 1991; Martin *et al.*, 1989). Ridgeway (1990) studied therapist variables as predictors of counselling effectiveness and concluded that multi-faceted empathy, purpose in life and self efficacy had a significant relationship with outcome measures of effectiveness, counsellor skill and client satisfaction.

One of the generic competencies that is universally sought from potential counsellors is self awareness. Most trainers would agree with Reik (1948) that the process of listening to one's own inner thoughts and feelings is a good training ground for hearing those of others. Allen (1967) explored the effectiveness of counsellor trainees as a function of psychological openness. He found a direct relationship between the freedom with which subjects responded to the Rorschach test (RIRS) (Levine and Spivack, 1964) and the competence assessment made by supervisors for each one. Self awareness, openness to own feelings and psychological mindedness contribute to emotional well-being, another factor that warrants attention during selection.

EMOTIONAL WELL-BEING

Clearly, to be able to sustain a counselling relationship with a range of clients presenting diverse problems, the counsellor must be able to distinguish their own emotions from those of their clients, to contain their own emotions sufficiently to give full attention to the client and to think clearly about material presented by them in order to make meaningful interventions. Carkhuff (1969), after much research on therapist variables, concluded that counsellors must be emotionally at least one step ahead of their clients. The implication is that they should have confronted their own areas of difficulty and be aware of what they are, even if they are not fully resolved. They must also be open to seeking support, whether that be personal therapy, through supervision or in consultation with peers, so that their emotional response to clients or others can be processed. Research efforts to link emotional well-being with counselling competence have been less than sufficient, partly due to the methodological complexities of designing outcome measures and the collection of outcome data. The evidence in general supports the suggestion that emotionally healthy therapists are associated with better outcomes for their clients (Bergin and Garfield, 1994).

More specifically, Wogan (1970) found that less effective therapists (as measured by outcome) had a tendency to deny their own negative personality characteristics, which supports the importance of openness to positive and negative personal qualities as well as for personal strengths and weaknesses. Garfield and Bergin (1971) used MMPI (Minnesota Multiphasic Personality Inventory) profiles on therapists and found that those with the lowest scores (hence lowest in emotional disturbance) were most effective in facilitating decreasing depression and defensiveness in their clients. Using patients' willingness to stay in therapy as an outcome measure (unreliable as it is), Anchor (1977) found therapist personality integration to be positively associated with good attendance for sessions.

PSYCHOLOGICAL MINDEDNESS

Psychological mindedness is described by Coltart (1993) as crucial if clients are to make use of psychoanalytic psychotherapy. If it is necessary for clients using this model, it must also be required of their therapists. Coltart lists nine qualities that she suggests add up to psychological mindedness, which she looks for when assessing patients for psychotherapy. They are (p.72):

- An acknowledgement, tacit or explicit, by the patient that he has an unconscious mental life, and that it affects his thoughts and behaviour.
- The capacity to give a self-aware history, not necessarily in chronological order.
- The capacity to give his history without prompting from the assessor, and with some sense of the patients' emotional relatedness to the events of his own life and their meaning for him.
- The capacity to recall memories, with their appropriate affects.
- Some capacity to take the occasional step back from his own story and to reflect upon it, often with the help of a brief discussion with the assessor.
- Signs of a willingness to take responsibility for himself and his own personal evolution.
- Imagination, as expressed in imagery, metaphors, dreams, identifications with other people, empathy, and so on.
- Some signs of hope and realistic self-esteem. This may be faint, especially if the patient is depressed, but it is nevertheless important.
- The overall impression of the development of the relationship with the assessor.

Counsellors themselves may be clients (although not necessarily for analysis) at some time during their training, another reason for seeking these qualities in potential trainees. They must be able to work therapeutically, whether as recipients or therapists. Guy (1987) concurs with Coltart's emphasis on the way in which family history is related, with his observation that family factors and early experiences are important when assessing suitability for training as a therapist, specifically in the way that they are recounted rather than their severity. Coltart (1988) comments that potential clients must be able to take responsibility for themselves, their thoughts, feelings and actions. Blaming others, lack of opportunity, bad luck or misfortune would be judged more negatively by an assessor than recognition of having made mistakes, missed opportunities or avoided risk taking. Counsellors must also take responsibility for their own thoughts, feelings and experiences in order to keep their own emotional world separate from that of their clients. A person-centred theoretical orientation would not concur with Coltart's suggestions, particularly with respect to recognizing unconscious processes.

OTHER FACTORS

In discussion with counsellor trainers various other aspects of suitability for counselling training were raised. Firstly there was general agreement that ideally candidates should be aged between thirty and fifty-five and selection of either older or younger trainees needed careful consideration. There was reluctance to consider people much below the age of thirty unless they demonstrated exceptional maturity. Reflection on life experience forms part of counselling training and adds an important dimension in considering the experience of others. Over the age of fifty-five, candidates might be considered after detailed consideration of their motivation to train for a new profession. Sexton and Whiston (1991), in a review of literature on counselling training, found no evidence to suggest that therapist age influences outcome of counselling. There is a concern that older people might be less amenable to personal growth and development and less able to manage change.

Secondly, the question of sex of counsellor was considered. In Britain many more women than men apply for counselling training courses. There is little evidence to suggest any difference between the effectiveness of male and female therapists (Atkinson and Shein, 1986) hence the major consideration in selection tends to be achieving some balance in the training group (see Stock-Whittaker, 1990, on selection for group therapy).

Thirdly in many instances candidates for counselling training from ethnic minorities are actively sought, as they are often under-represented on counselling courses.

Fourthly the selection of counsellors with strong religious beliefs was discussed. Few therapists believe that religious themes are within the province of psychotherapy (Bergin and Jensen, 1989) and attitudes towards the role of religion in the counselling relationship need to be carefully explored. There is no reason why someone with deeply held religious beliefs should not be able to help someone with different beliefs (Propst *et al.*, 1992) as long as the counsellor is able to contain their own beliefs and not impose them on their clients.

Finally there was an intense discussion about the selection of candidates with disabilities. Such disabilities might include blindness, physical disability, disfigurement, or degenerative illness. Little is known about the impact disabled counsellors have on clients. Wheeler (1996) gave an account of her work with a trainee counsellor, who suffered from a life threatening illness and who died in training. The trainee's resistance to acknowledging her rapidly declining health was seen as unhelpful for the relationships with clients who were shocked when she died. In general the counsellor trainers concluded that if a physically disadvantaged person met all the other criteria associated with selection and they could physically cope with the demands of the course then they should be accepted.

In a survey of counsellor training courses conducted by the author respondents were asked to list six criteria they considered to be the most important in selection of students. The criteria mentioned by the forty respondents have been grouped under the headings given in Table 3.1. This data was obtained by asking people to write down six criteria they considered to be important. The list given in Table 3.1 is a summary of the results.

Table 3.1 *Criteria considered to be important in the selection of counsellor trainees*

1.	Qualifications/degree/able to cope with academic content/ability to translate experience into the written word	27
2.	Personal qualities/maturity/imagination/intuition/openness/able to benefit from self development/ability to form a helping relationship	23
3.	Self awareness/insight/honesty/ability to make links	20
4.	Previous/current counselling experience	17
5.	Motivation	16
6.	Emotional stability and absence of personality disturbance	15
7.	Previous counselling training	14
8.	Awareness of course model and congruity with it	11
9.	Sound reasons for training not just personal development	9
10.	Experience of or willingness to engage in therapy	6
11.	Previous mental health work experience	6
12.	Other	6
13.	Ability to challenge and be challenged	4
14.	References	3
15.	Financial/time resources to meet costs	3
16.	Age	2
17.	Evidence of awareness of minority issues	1

The list of criteria for selection generated by the research mirrored the criteria that were discussed at the conference and that were described in interviews with trainers. The most frequently reported criterion was academic ability or ability to communicate ideas in writing, which may be skewed by the fact that over half the institutions in the sample were universities or institutes of higher education (79.4 per cent), although academic ability has been shown not to predict counselling competence (Nevid and Gildea, 1984). One study has investigated the relative effectiveness of trainees with or without a background in psychology. Sharpley and Ridgeway (1991) assessed trainees during a simulated interview following a five-week training programme in counselling. Those with a background in psychology achieved significantly higher scores for counselling skills than those without such a background.

The next most frequently reported criterion was related to personal qualities: maturity, openness, imagination, ability to form a helping relationship, closely followed by the need for self awareness, insight, honesty and the ability to make links between past and present. Emotional stability and absence of personality disturbance were considered important, as would be expected.

Previous experience was considered to be important for many of the respondents. Some required previous counselling training, or relevant work experience, others experience of personal therapy, but these requirements would vary depending on the type of course offered. More advanced courses would usually require previous experience whereas introductory courses demand less. Motivation and suitability for a particular course were criteria that respondents to the survey thought were important. Counselling training is in great demand but the motives of candidates seeking such training need to be explored. Counselling training is chosen by some as a substitute (consciously or unconsciously) for personal therapy, in the hope that the course will help resolve their own conflicts. While personal growth and development is often achieved through counsellor training, it should not be the prime motivating factor and trainees should also seek professional development.

Potential students need to have thought carefully about the kind of course they apply for. The theoretical stance taken by courses varies and each course will suit some people more than others. For example a potential student who applies for a psychodynamic course without reading any of the psychoanalytic literature to inform their decision might be considered unsuitable for acceptance as they have not made an informed choice. Other theoretical model courses may have similar expectations. One respondent to the survey wanted evidence that potential students have an awareness of minority issues. Undoubtably had a list of criteria been provided for respondents to choose from, this would have received more attention.

Finally a criterion for selection that received few mentions in the survey but a lot of comment in the discussion between trainers was that potential trainees should have time and resources to commit to the course. Counselling training is demanding both emotionally and in terms of time commitment. Unless a candidate has the financial resources to meet the fees and time to attend the course and devote to supervision, client work and private study, they will be unlikely to succeed.

The selection criteria described below are largely those described by Dryden *et al.* (1995) in their book *Issues in Professional Counsell or Training* written using their experience with the BAC course recognition group.

Criterion questions

1. Does the applicant have prior counselling experience?
2. Does the applicant have previous experience as a client of counselling or therapy?

3.   Does the applicant have prior experience of counselling or coun-
     selling skills training?
4.   Is the applicant more interested in counselling training as a means
     of personal growth or does she/he seriously want to enter the
     profession?
5.   Will the applicant be able to meet the academic challenges
     involved in the course?
6.   Is the course coming at the right time in the applicant's develop-
     ment as a counsellor?
7.   Is the applicant too old or too young for training?
8.   Does the applicant have a basic awareness of and compatibility
     with the core theoretical model of the course?
9.   Does the applicant have a personality which is inappropriate for
     counselling?

When selecting trainees, individuals may fit all the criteria agreed and
seem like the perfect candidates but what is unknown is how much they can
change as a result of the course, how they learn and how much they can
learn. The ideal candidate may be the right age, academically able, self
aware, self confident, emotionally expressive, able to conceptualize, have a
good clinical memory, the right previous experience and good rapport with
others, but fail to engage with the learning environment of the course and
the core model offered. On the other hand counsellors need maturity,
psychological adjustment and emotional well being, but whether these have
to be there at the beginning of training is questionable (Strupp *et al.*, 1988).
Selectors can only be 'good enough' in selecting what they hope will be
'good enough' counsellors and accept that they are unlikely to get it right
100 per cent of the time.

THE PROCESS OF SELECTION

The process of selection varies between institutions (Purton, 1991) but also
depends on the theoretical orientation that a course offers. Some courses
favour a formal and perhaps deliberately intimidating selection process
while others will choose to be more informal and involve an element of self
selection.

APPLICATION FORMS

The process usually starts with an application form. The information
sought by such means will vary according to the intensity of the next stage
of the process. One participant in the trainers' discussion group mentioned
that he had refined his application form to such an extent that he no longer
needed to conduct face to face interviews. He made his selection from the

forms submitted and was satisfied with the results. Although this practice was envied by some as selection interviewing is time consuming, most trainers saw the interview process as essential.

Ingram and Zurawski (1981) suggested that an application form for counselling training should include a personal autobiography, a statement of purpose, a self assessment statement as well as biographical information. Purton (1991) quotes an interview with Paul Keeble, in which he describes the selection process for WPF training courses which requires a detailed autobiographical statement for which candidates are assisted by a set of guidelines. The statement asks for details of early life experiences, and significant life events and is similar to the kind of questionnaires issued to prospective psychotherapy patients by some clinics. Such application forms are not intended to screen out candidates who have had difficult life experiences. The questions give the selector an indication of how self aware the applicant is and later at interview stage the extent to which life events have been assimilated and managed can be judged. Some people have had traumatic experiences through which they have worked and from which they have grown and developed. Others have had similar experiences that have been denied or buried, that cannot be talked about and have not been resolved. Selectors may be wary of applicants who are unable to view their lives objectively or who are completely devoid of any emotion accompanying significant disclosures. The person-centred course mentioned by Purton did not require such detailed application information, consistent with a person-centred model which places less emphasis on the past.

REFERENCES

References from other professionals with intimate knowledge of the candidates' work are usually sought, although reference letters (Guy, 1987) have been shown to be uncritical and poor predictors of counselling competence. Empirical evidence from a study by Baxter *et al.* (1981) demonstrated that references did not reveal discriminative, consensual or differentiating patterns of perception of candidates. However anecdotal evidence suggests that poor references can be extremely valuable in giving information about candidates, particularly with respect to candidates' self awareness, perception and relationships with others. Unless required to ask for a reference from a particular person, candidates usually choose referees who will view them positively. It can be valuable to spot a referee that a candidate might have chosen but has not, such as an employer, supervisor or previous training course tutor. Anecdotal evidence suggests that references should always be sought from the previous course when students seek to transfer. There may be legitimate reasons for the transfer but such references can illuminate potential difficulties that may influence the decision to accept the applicant.

INTERVIEWS

Most counsellor training courses will use a selection interview, which BAC course recognition guidelines recommend (1996) be conducted by two interviewers. The structure and content of the interviews varies between courses. For instance the FDI person-centred course quoted in Purton (1991) states, 'The interview provides an opportunity to assess applicants' empathic capabilities. To what extent are they able to be sensitive to the interviewers in a situation which naturally encourages self centredness?' (p.38). The interview is also a forum 'to check on: (a) the applicant's capacity for theoretical study . . . (b) awareness of the effects that the course may have on his or her domestic life' (p.38); also '(c) that the course can be managed financially; (d) that the prime motive for doing the course is for training rather than personal development; (e) that the course has been purposely chosen for its orientation'.

The University of London, MSc course (quoted in the same chapter) focuses on different issues in the interview namely that (a) applicants are committed to train for a career in counselling; (b) that they have had some personal growth experience; (c) that they have read some relevant counselling literature; (d) that they can discuss their own strengths and weaknesses. The interview is designed to be challenging in order to assess the candidate's performance under pressure. Another interview technique used by psychodynamic courses is to include a trial interpretation about personal material revealed in the interview to gauge the interviewee's response. If the interpretation is heard and considered it may be an indication of their ability to work with psychodynamic ideas, whereas if it is rejected outright, that may indicate resistance. It is none the less a challenge to the applicant to which their response will be observed. Interviews should not be therapy sessions but as Coltart (1988) concludes, the way in which people relate their history and past experience says a lot about their psychological mindedness.

The fourth course described by Purton is a diploma in psychosynthesis. As is sometimes the case with other courses, here students are required to take an introductory course prior to applying for the diploma course. Two interviewers, who are not involved in assessment on the introductory course, see candidates with the evaluation sheets from that course at their disposal. Criteria used for selection include 'previous professional training and experience, ability to form a helping relationship, openness to the transpersonal, capacity to deal effectively with the psychological and cognitive demands of the course, self-awareness, maturity and the ability to function co-operatively in a group with awareness and sensitivity' (p.40).

The selectors use a rating scale constructed around the criteria mentioned above to make decisions about applicants.

Nevid and Gildea (1984) have written about the selection of candidates for clinical psychology training for which a five-point rating scale ranging from poor to excellent was employed after an interview. Sixty candidates were interviewed by two faculty members who could structure interviews as they wished. The following qualities were rated: research potential; clinical potential; verbal skills/fluency; interpersonal skills and overall evaluation. The inter-relationships between these variables and other variables related to academic performance were subjected to a step-wise multiple discriminate analysis to examine the relative contributions of all the variables to accepted, waiting list and rejected candidates. Clinical potential was the most highly weighted measure among the interview ratings. The interview variables were highly inter-correlated. It was concluded that the interview evaluations contributed more to the discrimination that lead to selection, waiting list or rejection than the academic records. Interviewer judgements were consistent across the measures. These were interesting results because of the attention focused on measuring interview performance. However this research did not deal with validity of interview measures to predict competence and success. Also the interviewers were not necessarily well trained to select clinicians, particularly with respect to their skill in predicting clinical potential.

INTERVIEWERS

This last statement highlights the issue of who the interviewers should be. Ideally they should be core course staff who will have to live with the decisions that they make. They should be clinicians, skilled in assessing clients' suitability for counselling. Some courses encourage self selection, providing information and an induction process to enable students to make an informed choice. This is quite a common occurrence for entry to the first stage of a counselling training programme when the gate-keeping function is performed at the end of the first year. Even then some courses will allow students to proceed on the basis of their self and peer assessment. Dijkstra (1986) proposed a procedure for selecting Rogerian therapy trainees with an emphasis on self selection. She maintains that a preliminary self selection procedure has a positive effect on the outcome of a training programme and the therapist's professional practice. Proctor (1984) ran a highly successful counselling training programme for many years at South West London College for which candidates selected themselves. The staff existed primarily to hold the boundaries of the course and to be a resource for learning. It was described as a self directed learning community.

OTHER TECHNIQUES USED TO ASSESS SUITABILITY

Group interviews

Some courses use a group interview or experience either instead of or in addition to individual interviews. Purton (1991) describes the WPF selection procedure which includes a one-day assessment, part of which is spent in groups of eight discussing a prepared case with a facilitator present. Assessment is made not only of ability to think about client material but also about the way individuals relate to each other in a group. Behaviour is observed and note taken of leadership qualities, ability to listen to others or to contribute in the group environment. The selection process for another course includes a group event during which candidates are given five topics to discuss for seventy-five minutes while a member of the course team observes the process. A rating scale is used to quantify the contribution made to the group in terms of openness, taking appropriate space, being supportive to and encouraging of others, listening to the contributions of others and making relevant comments that demonstrate understanding of aspects of counselling or the counselling process. Topics such as: Can counsellors change people?; Are there any conflicts between counselling and religion?; Can everyone benefit from counselling?; Can confidentiality be guaranteed for all clients?; Should all counsellors have their own personal therapy and if so why?; are included on a discussion sheet distributed to all participants. Such an exercise provides an excellent opportunity to assess performance in a group and regularly highlights potential problems, such as being unable to listen to others, that are not apparent in individual interviews.

More selection ideas

While not suggesting that there is likely to be any reliable alternative to a face to face interview in selecting suitable candidates for counsellor training, what follows is a review of some of the ideas and suggestions that have been put forward by various authors that might contribute to the overall system of selection. These include tests and exercises of varying degrees of complication that might be administered on a selection day with the aim of discriminating between likely candidates. When there is fierce competition for places, final decisions between good applicants are difficult without an objective measure.

McLeod and McLeod (1993) have suggested that an exercise such as the Helping Relationship Incident (Combs and Soper, 1963) could be usefully employed in the selection of counsellors. The exercise involves writing about a helping relationship incident that was deemed to be positive, which is subsequently rated on twelve dimensions of counsellor 'perceptual organization'. Combs and Soper concluded that a person-centred perceptual organization or belief system is an important factor in counsellor effectiveness, which can be measured using this instrument. In the same article McLeod and McLeod review literature relating to the topic of personal philosophy, attitudes and perceptual organization of counsellors that influence effectiveness. They also discuss cognitive flexibility as defined by Whiteley *et al.* (1967) which is the ability to think and act simultaneously and appropriately in a given situation. Cognitive flexibility has been positively correlated with supervisor ratings of ability. Whiteley suggested that a measure of cognitive flexibility is useful in the selection of counsellors because it is not easily influenced through training. Students who are diagnosed to be cognitively inflexible are unlikely to change and are hence less likely to make good counsellors.

Sharpley *et al.* (1994) have developed a 'standardized client' procedure for assessing the impact of a counsellor trainee's behaviour on the rapport they develop with the client. A client is trained to present the same genuine concern to trainees in all interviews and to make minute by minute assessments of rapport. This is most relevant for the assessment of skills and will be discussed further in Chapter 4, but a variation on this system can also be used for selection. It could provide a measure of the potential student's ability to develop a therapeutic alliance and engage the client effectively. The process produces an overall score which can be used to discriminate between one candidate and another.

Sharpley and his colleagues have looked at various other methods of predicting performance in counsellors. In 1993, Sharpley and Ridgeway published an article relating to self efficacy as a predictor of trainees' counselling skills performance. Measurements of self efficacy were taken before, midway and at the end of a counselling skills course. There were no significant findings overall to suggest that self efficacy predicts final results, but a measure of self efficacy taken midway through the course was negatively correlated with the level of skill finally achieved. In other words, trainees who underestimated their ability were rated higher on their skills performance at the end of the course.

In the 1970s Nelson-Jones and Patterson (1975) developed a counsellor attitude scale as an instrument for measuring client centredness. The scale has seventy items, statements to which respondents can agree or disagree, such as, 'The counsellor's goal is to make people better adjusted to society' or 'It is not the job of the counsellor to solve people's problems' (p.233). Administering the scale to students after counsellor training, scores on the counsellor attitude scale were found to predict students' ability to demonstrate empathy. Other writers have suggested that a battery of psychological tests be used as part of the selection process (Holt and Luborsky, 1958), with the possible addition of a psychiatric interview. In a review of literature about counsellor characteristics and effectiveness, Rowe *et al.* (1975) highlighted various studies that sought to find a relationship between the Sixteen Personality Factor questionnaire (16PF) and desirable counsellor characteristics. While one study by Donnan, Harlan and Thompson (1969) found that Factor A (outgoing, warm-hearted) correlated significantly with unconditional positive regard, Factor C (emotional stability) correlated with congruence and Factor H (venturesome) correlated with trust, these results were not replicated in other studies. The field seems to be wide open for the development of reliable tests to predict success on counsellor training courses and subsequent counsellor competence.

Residential selection programmes

There has been a recent trend in selection for management positions to organize residential selection programmes spanning two on three days. Typically such a programme will include exercises, aptitude tests and interviews as well as providing opportunities for informal discussion and observation of candidates' interpersonal and other behaviour (Bray, 1982). 'It has been found that the validity of recruitment decisions made from assessment centre data is much higher than that obtained from interview or individual tests' (McLeod, 1992). It may be true that good recruitment decisions have been made from such programmes but the advantages and disadvantages are fairly obvious. In favour of such programmes is the opportunity for in-depth assessment of personality factors, skills, abilities and aptitudes. Against, is the huge time and financial commitment for staff and participants. On balance the most advantageous method of selection for a substantial counselling training course may be through a screening process at the end of the first year of training. Given that the most promising students may not fulfil their potential and some who start with a low level of skill may become stars, it offers opportunities for all, although at the end of that first year there may be disappointments.

COPING WITH REJECTION

Whether at the end of such an introductory year or after a standard interview process, there will be students or potential students who are disappointed, upset and angry. 'We must improve our methods for retaining students and removing students from our programmes who cannot be helpful to clients. Counsellor educators directly influence the counselling services provided by the quality of counsellors they train' (Sexton and Whiston, 1991, p.4).

Opinions vary as to whether candidates should be offered any feedback when they are unsuccessful in gaining a place on a course. When they have already participated in one year of a course it is likely that they will have received regular feedback on their performance so that the final decision that they should not proceed will be less of a shock. Nevertheless they may be angry and disappointed. The most difficult students to discourage from continuing with counselling training are typically those who most need to be discouraged. They will be students who can either not hear or make use of critical feedback. They tend towards being narcissistic and perceive any negatively phrased comment as a personal attack, against which they defend with denial or projection. Hence they either ignore the comments and cannot learn from them or perceive the trainer as bad and unskilled and hence unworthy of passing any judgement (for more on such students see Chapter 7).

Whether it is decided to give feedback or not must be consistent practice, backed by policy decisions to avoid discriminatory practice. For example one course team decided that feedback would be made available after interviews to unsuccessful candidates but only in response to a written request. Feedback would then be returned in writing. Experiences of talking to distraught candidates on the telephone informed this policy decision. The feedback itself is often difficult to phrase because rejection decisions have been made subjectively based on personal response to the person and aspects of their personality or interpersonal behaviour. Feedback is more easily given when it relates to academic issues or scores in a test, which may be a good reason to include some form of test or rating scale in the interview process.

An alternative strategy is to adopt a policy of giving no feedback at all. This may be more comfortable for the trainers concerned but will leave unsuccessful candidates wondering about their failure.

CONCLUSION

Selection on to a course is the first and most crucial step towards counselling competence. The aim of all institutions will be to ensure that their students have the best possible chance of success in the course they undertake. Counselling competence is not achieved through academic study alone. A student could read every book on counselling available, write excellent essays and yet be quite unsuitable and unskilled for clinical practice. Who they are, how they relate to others, how they conceptualize clients' difficulties, how they manage their own concerns, are all crucial to counselling competence, and these aspects of counselling course candidates must be assessed at the outset. It is for trainers to devise the best possible system with the resources available to select trainees who can go on to achieve success.

FOUR

Assessing competence: ways and means

Having selected the best possible candidates for a counsellor training programme, the task of delivering an appropriate package of learning and assessment experiences begins, although considerable thought will have been given to the desired outcome for students. The practice of student-centred learning is now widespread and learning outcomes in general terms or target competencies in more specific terms should be documented and discussed at the beginning of the course. Students need to know what is expected of them in order to direct their learning and monitor their own progress towards the final goal, using feedback from tutors, peers and others along the way.

Despite criticisms of the NVQ developments in assessing counselling competence (Foskett, 1994), a brief glance at the standards that have been developed quickly informs the reader about target competencies, breadth of competence, performance criteria, knowledge specification and evidence requirements involved. The NVQ scheme has been rigorously developed using a vast amount of expertise and has produced a sophisticated product that courses will find increasingly difficult to ignore. Its impact may force all courses to either adopt the NVQ standards or to re-evaluate their own objectives and criteria for assessment, to produce targets that are clearly defined and measurable. Coupled with this development is the growing body of evidence (Roswell, 1993) that we are following the trend in the USA towards a more litigious society with the inevitable consequence that greater attention must be paid to procedures that will stand up to investigation in the event of complaint. The BAC Complaints Panel already receives a considerable number of complaints related to courses, some of which refer to assessment procedures.

Setting target competencies or learning outcomes for a training experience is a complex task. It has to take account of the level of competence students are expected to have when they embark on a course and the amount of time and other resources available to produce the desired outcome. The objectives must be realistic and attainable. They must take account of the kind of employment trainees are likely to seek at the end of the course and of standards imposed by professional organizations such as BAC, BPS, COSCA or UKCP. Given that BAC accreditation requires that applicants had in excess of 450 hours of training or substantial counselling experience, it would be unrealistic to expect students to have achieved a high level of professional competence after only 200 hours of training. Further, while there will be generic competencies common to most counselling training courses there will also be specific aspects of knowledge or skills that pertain to the core therapeutic orientation of the course or to client groups on which the course is focused.

EXAMPLES OF COMPETENCIES USED BY TWO DIFFERENT COURSES

The Communication and Counselling Foundation is a private organization that offers a Diploma in Integrative Psychosynthesis Counselling based in London and Worcester. The course is part-time spread over three years and target competencies have been identified for each of the three years, as listed below:

Year 1

The ability to:
- demonstrate a commitment to on-going personal development
- conduct an initial interview and evaluate clients in relation to the intake guidelines – establish a counselling frame with a clear contract which includes time, space and money boundaries
- establish a clear relationship where the counsellor's intention is explicit and shared
- communicate genuineness, empathy and unconditional positive regard
- make genuine/congruent interventions
- accurately reflect what the client in communicating using their words
- listen to both the words and the energy behind their words
- recognize and stand back from one's own feelings and thoughts and be able to distinguish them from the client's experience
- have an understanding of the psychosynthesis theoretical model and be able to use this model to understand the process of the client
- understand the context of abuse and deprivation and its consequences on the client and to be able to view the client from this context

- demonstrate an ability to be open to feedback from peers and trainers in supervision and in general

Year 2

The ability to:
- build on the competencies of Year 1
- formulate and hold a hypothesis about the client from the information communicated
- make interventions informed by hypotheses
- make interpretative interventions from hypotheses
- work from the context of self realization
- dis-identify from the counselling process and see the whole or gestalt
- develop rapport
- recognize, take responsibility for and work with countertransference
- understand the effects of cultural context on the client
- see the client's issues in the larger context of their life journey as a whole

Year 3

The ability to:
- build on the competencies of Years 1 and 2
- assess clients in relation to the intake guideline
- formulate a hypothesis from information communicated both consciously and unconsciously
- work with and evoke unconscious material through dream and imagery
- work through interpretation of the transference
- work with the countertransference both authentically and interpretatively
- carry out one's own research
- extrapolate from one's own work with clients and research and articulate understanding and ideas
- demonstrate that the trainee can build and integrate a personal model for counselling (especially in the long essay)
- demonstrate that the model can be used in clinical work (especially the end of the year session tape)
- develop an I-Thou relationship
- be a stable and containing presence
- build and maintain a counselling practice

Reproduced in full with kind permission from Kate Vickers and Hilary Thompson (1995)

The course evaluates competence through the use of tutorials, essays, supervision and the evaluation of a work file which includes course notes, supervision notes, presentation materials, essays, clinical notes and notes of self evaluation sessions. In-depth interviews with course staff are conducted each year in which target competencies are identified and discussed.

By contrast the two-year post graduate diploma in counselling practice at the Isis Centre in Oxford (validated by Oxford Brookes University) is a psychodynamic course. Students accepted on to the course have prior experience of counselling training and practice and are expected to achieve a high level of competence by its completion. Only a small number of students form each cohort and they work closely with the staff team, offering a counselling service to the general public, at the centre. The course defines learning outcomes for their students in general terms as:

- clarification of models of the mind
- theories of human development
- clinical learning outcomes – counselling (see specific competencies)
- assessment of clients
- general learning outcomes (e.g. working with a team)
- personal growth and development

Specific clinical competencies to be achieved and demonstrated are listed below. The course states that although these are clinical competencies, theoretical understanding should be integrated and demonstrated through the work with clients.

1. The initial contact and its management
   Students will be able to demonstrate competence to:
   a. assess the suitability of a client for counselling;
   b. manage the counselling setting in a way that shows under-standing of its therapeutic significance;
   c. form an initial counselling relationship with a client;
   d. negotiate a counselling contract with a client;
   e. find a focus for the counselling work;
   f. establish a working alliance with a client;
   g. choose between individual, couple and group therapy;
   h. understand the neurotic/psychotic boundary and its clinical implications.

2. The counselling work
   Students will be able to demonstrate the ability to:
   a. recognize the significance of boundary issues in the clinical work;
   b. receive a history and understand its significance;

c. recognize transference phenomena and their clinical relevance;

d. recognize counter-transference phenomena and their clinical relevance;

e. contain a client's expression of painful emotion and behaviour;

f. in keeping with 2e, recognize and respond appropriately to suicidal and other destructive ideas;

g. respond appropriately to questions about the counsellor and understand issues concerning self disclosure;

h. look for meaning in enactment by clients, e.g. in being early or late, missing appointments, seeking contact between appointments;

i. recognize and work with the meaning for clients of the beginning and end of each session, the intervals between sessions, holiday breaks and absences;

j. recognize defence mechanisms and their relevance to clinical material, management and treatment;

k. In keeping with 2j, understand the concepts of repetition compulsion and working through as it relates to the counselling tasks;

l. work with short- and long-term clients;

m. recognize limitations of self, client and setting;

n. link material from past and present and here and now;

o. time interpretations;

p. work with clients of differing ages, gender, background and culture, and understand the significance for client and counsellor of counsellor-client difference;

q. work with dream material and other unconscious derivatives;

r. negotiate an ending appropriately;

s. understand and work with the issues relating to matters of follow up and referral on.

3. Psychodynamic processes

Students will be able to demonstrate ability to understand and work with the psychodynamic processes which may underlie the following:

a. the effects of bereavement and loss;

b. the effects of trauma and its relationship to post traumatic stress disorder;

c. the effects of sexual abuse in childhood;

d. the effects of physical abuse in childhood;

e. the effects of physical illness;

the presentation of:

f. anxiety symptoms;

g. experiences of depression;

h. psychosomatic symptoms and problems;

 i. sexual dysfunction;
 j. relationship problems and problems in the forming and sustaining of relationships;
 k. eating disorders;
 l. obsessive symptoms;
 m. marital and family problems;
 n. problems relating to stages in the life cycle.

The competencies described relate specifically to psychodynamic practice. Each competence is further refined by statements of a level of competence, understanding and skill at various assessment points throughout the course. For example 2: 'recognize defence mechanisms and their relevance to clinical material, management and treatment.' After four months: 'students should have an awareness of these psychodynamic concepts and be aware of their use by reflection on client material during supervision.' After one year: 'students should be able to recognize the use of defence mechanisms and differentiate between neurotic defences and more primitive methods and use such differentiation in assessment.' After two years: 'students should be aware of each client's defence strategies and make good judgements about challenging or not; they can use their perceptions to assess the nature of the work to be undertaken.' At these stages, assessment is based on course members' presentation of self assessment, assessment by their tutor and supervisor and on the course member's journal work. In addition case studies, essays and seminar presentation contribute to the overall assessment. (Extracts reproduced with permission from Patrick Parry Okeden, Oxford Brookes University and the Isis Centre, Oxfordshire Mental Health Care NHS Trust, Oxford OX1 2HS.

 Inevitably courses will produce target competencies that match the values, beliefs and competencies of the staff involved. To produce a comprehensive and exhaustive list of detailed competencies would be a daunting task, as the experience of volunteer professionals engaged in the definition of competencies for National Vocational Qualifications have found (see Chapter 8).

 With a set of learning outcomes and target competencies to work towards, a course can be designed to facilitate learning, understanding and the development of skill in a multitude of different ways. A system will be devised to confirm that trainees have achieved the desired competencies by the end of the course and ideally to inform students of their progress on their way. This would be described as a system for formative and summative assessments. Many factors will influence the final system, not least the amount of time available to engage in assessment from both a staff and student perspective.

 The American Association for Counseling and Development have published a manual of counsellor competencies, performance guidelines and assessment (Engels and Dameron, 1990). The manual itemizes specific counselling competencies for selected environments and populations in- cluding: addiction counselling, counselling for adolescents and children, counselling in higher education, mental health settings, schools, counselling for individuals, couples, families and groups. An extract is reproduced here to give an example of the detail that is involved (pp.53–5):

INDIVIDUAL COUNSELLING

Goal Statement: The professional counsellor develops, maintains and provides effective counselling skills that help clients grow towards personal goals and strengthen their capacity to cope with life situations.

Competencies: The counsellor is a skilled professional who is able to:

1. Demonstrate an understanding of the basic principles of human growth and development and how they affect the counselling process.

Performance guidelines: The professional counsellor provides evidence of competence by demonstrating the ability to:

1.1 describe the fundamental principles of individual development (physical, cognitive, emotional, moral, social and spiritual) through the life span;
1.2 explain the family life cycle and its effects on individual behaviour;
1.3 assess client's developmental levels and development issues;
1.4 communicate effectively with clients of different ages and developmental levels;

2. Understand and explain how cultural variations affect the counselling process:

2.1 explain the value, mores and behavioural patterns associated with various cultural or sub-cultural groups represented by both the counsellor and individual clients;
2.2 cite basic physical and psychological needs and cultural universals that constitute a basis for commonality between all humans;
2.3 asses the extent to which membership in or affiliation with a particular culture or subculture affects the values and behaviour of both the counsellor and individual clients;
2.4 increase awareness of personal prejudices regarding racism, sexism, ageism, and/or poverty, and attempt to relinquish such prejudices;

2.5 develop counselling techniques to bridge cultural differences that may exist between counsellor and client;

3. Explain the major counselling theories and their associated procedures and techniques:

3.1 For each major theory explain the following in the vocabulary associated with that theory:

3.1a philosophical assumptions;

3.1b view of human nature, including innate drives and tendencies for all humans;

3.1c personality development and structure;

3.1d etiology of maladaptive behaviour;

3.1e assessment of clients;

3.1f necessary and sufficient conditions under which psychological growth and/or behavioural change can or will occur;

3.1g specific procedures and techniques that facilitate constructive client change;

3.1h rationale for differential treatment based on a client's developmental level, cultural affiliation or problem(s);

3.2 identify commonalities and differences among the major counselling theories;

3.3 specify limitations of each major counselling theory;

3.4 explain how each major theory would conceptualize and treat a given case example.

The manual suggests that counsellors should be assessed on a scale of 1–5 for each of the performance guidelines listed. What the manual does not offer is any assistance in determining just how the performance guidelines should be measured. It is immediately apparent from the sample competencies described in this system that either knowledge of major theoretical models is very shallow, in which case it would be difficult to satisfy all the performance guidelines, or that counsellors would have to engage in a long period of training to acquire the knowledge and experience necessary.

WHAT HAS TO BE ASSESSED?

Taking the author's model (illustrated in Chapter 2), essential elements that contribute towards counsellor competence include self awareness, awareness of the client, the relationship, the therapeutic frame and environmental issues. However aspects of competence may be difficult to measure discretely and ultimately the crucial test is whether a range of clients achieve positive outcomes as a result of their experience with a particular counsellor and whether that level of performance can be sustained. While there is no reason that feedback from clients should not be used in the assessment of competence, the methodological difficulties inherent in measuring outcome and the amount of time and effort involved in achieving such measures are likely to mitigate against final or even summative assessment being concluded by these means. Hence the tendency is for assessment systems to be devised using a range of instruments, assignments, reports, discussions and technological interventions that attempt to simulate a picture of what the candidate is like as a counsellor, which may include an assessment of their own psychological functioning and interpersonal skills.

It is this last statement that assessment of the counsellor includes assessment of the person that makes counselling training different from other professional training courses. It is painful to be unsuccessful in any assessment process but it is particularly distressing when there are personal implications. Hence the assessment process requires a greater degree of sensitivity and support than might otherwise be the case. Students often experience assessment as threatening and suffer considerable stress when they do not do well. This has to be taken into account when thinking about appropriate methods of assessment. For this and other reasons an assessment procedure that hinges only on tasks performed at the end of the course is likely to be unsuitable for counsellor training and some form of on-going or interim assessment will at least provide opportunities for the discussion of weaknesses and possibly referral for counselling or psychotherapy or other remedial help where necessary. Klein and Babineau (1974) wrote about evaluating the competence of trainees as being 'nothing personal' (p.788). They identified the threatening nature of assessment of clinical competence in trainee psychiatrists and made a series of recommendations to institutions including the following:

1. Decide whether evaluations are necessary and if so for what purposes. The value of accomplishing these purposes should be weighed against the costs involved, e.g. expenditure of time, money, energy and educational resources.
2. Determine whether the evaluation process constitutes a formal part of the training programme. If so evaluations should be put in writing and shown to trainees for comments. Formative and summative evaluations should be provided at specified intervals.

Formative and summative assessments may include tests of knowledge in a pure (theoretical) or applied form, theoretical concepts applied to case material or aspects of clinical practice. Pure knowledge might be assessed as part of a formative process to encourage reading and assimilation of new material as well as the process of thinking about human development and theoretical concepts.

In the survey on assessment in counsellor training in Britain which informs aspects of this book, institutions offering counsellor training to diploma level or above were given a list of possible assessment methods of counselling competence and asked to indicate which they employed on their course. There was also a category for other means of assessment. The results are given in Tables 4.1 and 4.2.

Formative assessment methods of counselling skills
(that are used throughout the course to monitor progress)
Respondents could tick any number of items

Table 4.1 *Formative assessment methods of counselling skills*

Role play exercises	32
Video role play	21
Video of real counselling sessions	3
Audio tape of role play sessions	13
Audio tape of real sessions	12
Case study of client work	27
Process recording of session from memory	13
Supervision report	26
Written test/examination	2
Oral examination	2
Learning journal	17
Other	10
Valid cases: 38	

Summative assessment methods of counselling skills
(that are used as a final assessment of skill)
Respondents could tick any number of items

Table 4.2 *Summative assessment methods of counselling skills*

Role play exercises	16
Video role play	13
Video of real counselling sessions	3
Audio tape of role play sessions	11
Audio tape of real sessions	12
Case study of client work	25
Process recording of session from memory	11
Supervision report	21
Written test/examination	3
Oral examination	4
Learning journal	18
Other	16
Valid cases: 38	

Seventeen courses out of thirty-nine used some form of rating scale to assess counselling skills.

Information was also gathered about the assessment of theoretical knowledge, the results of which are given in Table 4.3.

Table 4.3 *Means of assessment of theoretical knowledge*

Case studies	30
Essays	35
Seminar presentation	17
Book reviews	1
Written examination	6
Oral examination	2
Other	6
Valid cases: 37	

Respondents were asked to give six criteria that they use to assess written work, the results of which are shown in Table 4.4.

Criteria for the assessment of written work
(In this question respondents could give criteria in their own words. Responses have been grouped under headings that were deduced from the responses given.)

Table 4.4 *Criteria for the assessment of written work*

Integration of insight with theoretical understanding	31
Awareness of core issues in counselling	23
Creativity/originality	11
Meet objectives, answer question set	19
Awareness of ethical/professional issues	11
Summarize appropriate material with references	15
Evidence of evaluation/good argument	20
Structure/clarity	26
Demonstrate an understanding of the process of counselling	13
Valid cases: 33	

WHAT ELSE MAY BE ASSESSED?

Aspects of competence may be assessed by varied means. Ethical and professional issues may be assessed by a written examination, verbally or through seminar presentation. They may also form part of a supervisor's feedback. The assessment of personal development is discussed fully in Chapter 6. Environmental awareness is more difficult to assess directly. Check lists for cross cultural counselling competence can be used, but it is more likely that society, organizational and contextual issues that affect counselling would be assessed through written work, indirectly through self and peer assessment exercises or via supervision.

WHO WILL ASSESS?

During the course of counsellor training there are a variety of people who come into contact with trainees who may be able to provide valuable information that can contribute to an assessment of competence. This includes the students themselves, course tutors, clinical supervisors, student peers, personal therapists, awareness group leaders, clients, placement manager or supervisor and the external assessor or examiner (McLeod, 1992). The choice of people to be involved in assessment will be influenced by the theoretical model of the course. For example a person-centred course will choose a self actualizing approach to assessment that will place more emphasis on self and peer evaluation than a psychodynamic course which will tend towards a more authoritarian, tutor led evaluation system. It is worth considering all of these potential sources of assessment, as they all have something to offer that can contribute to a comprehensive overview of counsellor performance, although low levels of agreement between competence ratings made by therapists, peers, trainers, supervisors and clients were found in a study by Chevron and Rounsaville (1983).

In the survey mentioned earlier in this chapter, the organizers of various courses were asked who contributed to the final assessment of student competence. The responses are given in Table 4.5.

[Respondents could choose up to three categories]

Table 4.5 Who makes the final assessment of student competence?

Student self assessment	20
Course staff	38
Peers	18
Client feedback	3
External examiner	25
Supervisor	13
Other	1
(39 respondents)	

COURSE STAFF

The staff of a substantial counselling course will get to know their students well and may be in a good position to assess the competence of trainees by the end of a course, but it will depend on the structure of the course and the roles and functions that staff fulfil. A staff team may include lecturers, personal tutors, clinical supervisors and group facilitators as well as external consultants. Some staff may be more concerned with the dissemination of knowledge and assessing academic standards than with clinical practice, and a team approach to assessment taking into account all perspectives could be beneficial. Target competencies have been discussed and there needs to be a comprehensive assessment system to ensure that all students are treated fairly. It is possible that there could be a personality clash between staff and student and safeguards against personal bias need to be included in the system. The use of standardized instruments for assessing competence can help to overcome these difficulties (see Chapter 5) although they too involve an element of subjectivity.

PLACEMENT MANAGER

Clinical practice is an essential part of training and trainees will usually have a placement with a counselling agency. Such an agency may or may not provide clinical supervision but will have someone who takes responsibility for work carried out. Such a person may not be a counsellor themselves but nevertheless can provide useful feedback. They will not be able to comment on work in sessions with clients but the placement manager should have an overview of the counsellor's performance, which would include client satisfaction and client attendance records. There is some evidence to suggest that client attendance rates correlate with competence as assessed by fellow trainees and supervisors (White and Pollard, 1982). Managers can also observe the counsellor's administrative capacity and relationship with other members of the placement team. McLeod (1992) cites Crandall and Allen (1982) who assert that the relationship between counsellors and their managers can mirror aspects of their relationships with clients. They should be able to comment on reliability and attendance, attitude towards clients and the counselling work and sense of commitment, as well as the counsellor's response to feedback and to authority. They may be able identify the counsellor's ability to recognize their weaknesses or their limitations with respect to their assessment of clients. It would be unrealistic to expect too much detailed feedback from a placement manager but a report commenting on the issues mentioned is crucial. It is in this domain that ethical and professional issues may be highlighted.

SUPERVISOR

The supervisor of a student's clinical work should have a clear sense of their competence. However assessment by a supervisor is fraught with difficulties. The supervisor is in a unique position of being close to the counsellor's work with clients. They are however only as close as the counsellor allows them to be. For example the counsellor has discretion over which clients they present for supervision and which aspects of sessions they discuss. It needs to be a space in which counsellors can discuss their thoughts, feelings, hunches, mistakes, concerns and dilemmas, fears and weaknesses. If an assessment element is added to the relationship it inhibits the free expression that is such a crucial element of the supervision process. Hence there is a fine balance between the desirability of using the insight gained through supervision for assessment purposes and the danger of contaminating a relationship that is the backbone of ethical clinical practice. The working alliance between the counsellor and supervisor may influence the assessment that is made of the trainee (Efstation *et al.*, 1990). Where the relationship is good the assessment may be more favourable. Stoltenberg and Delworth (1987) have discussed the developmental role of a supervisor which changes as counsellors gain experience and Davis (1989) has written about the problems of assessment through supervision. (Assessment through supervision is given more attention in Chapter 6.)

SELF ASSESSMENT

Once qualified and practising, counsellors are responsible for themselves and the service they provide for their clients. They must monitor and evaluate their practice and make crucial decisions when assessing clients, interacting in the counselling relationship and managing boundary, ethical and administrative issues. They need to work with their own internal supervisor (Casement, 1985) to reflect on the process of counselling and their understanding of client material. Although there will be a supervision arrangement which offers support and sometimes guidance, most of the counsellor's work is self regulated with accountability being to the client, and sometimes to an agency. Self assessment must be a part of every counsellor's repertoire and is essentially an on-going process. It is therefore highly desirable that students are encouraged to engage in self reflective processes, whether or not a formal self assessment is included in any summative decision about competence. Some courses will place more emphasis on self assessment than others. McLeod (1992) argues 'that counsellors in training may not know enough about good practice to be able to make accurate judgements of their own competence. On the other hand ... the ability to make such judgements should be one of the primary objectives of training courses' (p.363). Self assessment can be aided with the use of standardized instruments such as that produced by Larson *et al.*

(1992) (detailed in Chapter 5) and the use of learning journals discussed in Chapter 6.

PEER ASSESSMENT

Students on a counselling course get to know each other very well. They share the hopes and fears that a course inspires, the anxieties around assessment and the relief or despair when assignments are returned. They spend time discussing theories, issues and cases and often share skills exercises, role play clients for each other and attend group supervision. Course colleagues have a long-term overview of each other. Just as trainees need to develop their reflective and critical capacities for themselves, they can also refine their skills by observing others. Hence incorporating an element of peer assessment of competence can be a valuable process for all concerned. It may not be a comfortable experience, particularly when feedback is negative, but counselling itself is not always a comfortable process. If peer assessment is built into a course as a formative assessment process as well as contributing to a final assessment and the course culture supports and contains the challenge that is generated within the group it can make a substantial contribution to the learning environment. Peers will know a lot about students' interpersonal relationships and personality factors which contribute to overall competence, and peer assessment can perhaps most productively contribute to personal development and assessment of self, as will be discussed in Chapter 6. Peer supervision can be a useful vehicle for increasing student responsibility for self and peer assessment while refining their own skills of clinical judgement (Wagner and Smith, 1979).

THE CLIENT AS ASSESSOR

McLeod (1992) advocates a social constructionist approach to assessment of competence which takes account of the experience of everyone involved with the counsellor of which the client is one. The client's experience of the counsellor is from the perspective of the lay consumer, who is untutored in what to expect from a counsellor. However they can report on many aspects of their encounter with the counsellor, such as how comfortable they feel with them, whether they feel helped by the experience, whether they feel understood and whether they would recommend the counsellor to a friend or relative. It would be unrealistic to ask them to comment on specific skills or conformity to a particular model. Llewelyn et al. (1987) has researched helpful aspects of therapy as experienced by clients and counsellors and found little agreement between them on the events reported. Ponterotto and Furlong (1985) have reviewed rating scales for evaluation of counsellor effectiveness by clients which will be included in a discussion of rating scales in Chapter 5. In summary, while there are methodological difficulties in finding appropriate instruments for collecting client evaluations of counsellor competence, it is a task worth pursuing to achieve a multi-dimensional overview.

THERAPIST ASSESSMENT

While not a tradition in counselling training, an assessment of suitability for work as an analyst is sought from the trainee analyst's therapist or analyst. The psychotherapy profession seems to cope with this assessment practice although, as with assessment by supervisors, it would seem to be fraught with conflict and difficulty. The therapist report does not include detail of the trainee's material but does make a global statement about whether they are ready to practice. Not all counsellors have personal therapy and not all courses require it. There are occasions, when trainees seem particularly troubled or disturbed, that the opinion of a therapist close to the student could be most helpful. Unfortunately it is often when students are most distressed that they are least able to hear the feedback that they are given. If a therapist report were to be included in any assessment procedure it would be vital that this was made clear to all concerned before an agreement with a therapist is made. For further discussion of difficult students see Chapter 7.

EXTERNAL ACCOUNTABILITY

A counselling training community, staff and students, can be a rich, exciting and dynamic entity that generates its own energy, ideas and standards. However it is essential that a person or persons external to the course, probably called an external examiner and unconnected with it in any other way, is appointed to monitor the performance of trainees and to ensure that counselling competence is comparable with standards achieved in other institutions. The external examiner would normally approve the content and procedures of the assessment scheme and read, view, or listen to samples of students' work to ensure that they are being assessed fairly (BAC, 1995b). The external assessor has a crucial role in ensuring that students are assessed fairly, given that staff have intense relationships with their students in which opinions are formed that may affect the way in which work is assessed. The limitation of external examination is the amount of work that an examiner can reasonably be expected to review, a task undertaken by someone who is paid a nominal amount, probably employed by another instituton, whose time may be limited. External accountability is discussed further in Chapter 9.

FIVE

What to assess and how: methods of assessing competence

The complex mix of skill, knowledge and experience that contributes to counsellor competence has been a constant theme of this book. It is not surprising given that competence is defined in many different ways that there are also a multitude of methods, schemes, systems and technical devices to assess competence. This chapter provides an overview of some of these methods or instruments with a brief discussion of their strengths and weaknesses. It needs to be borne in mind that any assessment scheme is likely to be a package that consists of a number of elements that contribute to an overall picture of competence. It is a skill in itself to put a comprehensive package together that produces a realistic assessment of a student's ability without burdening them unduly with time consuming, anxiety provoking tasks that detract from the learning environment.

Overholser (1993) describes a five-component schema for defining competence which include factual knowledge, generic clinical skills, orientation specific technical skill, clinical judgement and interpersonal attributes. The components described in Chapter 2 used the five domains of self, other, relationship, therapeutic frame and environmental considerations. While some may argue that competence can be assessed solely through clinical practice, it would take a vast amount of assessed practice to ensure that clinical judgement was always reliable, environmental issues were sufficiently accounted for, professional ethics were understood and consistently adhered to and that personal concerns were always dealt with outside the counselling relationship. Reference will be made here to the assessment of theoretical knowledge, counselling skills, professional ethics, professional and self development, interpersonal relationships as well as clinical competence.

TREATMENT MANUAL

McLeod (1995) has identified five sources of difficulty in defining compe-tence that take account of interactive and systemic dimensions of a counsel-lor's practice, which are the flexibility of the counselling role, the complex-ity of the counselling task, the difficulty of accessing examples of counsellor behaviour related to real clients, the complexities of measuring outcome with clients, and the influence of the context in which counselling takes place. He describes two strategies that try to address the inherent difficul-ties, the use of a manualized therapy or a taxonomy of skills. The manu-alized therapy prescribes specific modes of intervention with a particular client group, while the taxonomy of skills attempts to identify core skills for any model and add to it modes of intervention that relate to an identified theoretical model.

Treatment manuals have been developed as an attempt to standardize practice and provide a pure form of treatment that will contribute to comparability and reliability in research studies that seek to explore and draw conclusions about the impact that counselling has on clients. The manual details all aspects of the therapeutic process including the therapist stance, contract with the client, duration of treatment, modes of response and information given to the client. Counsellors are trained to follow the manual and adherence to the manual is monitored through the use of tape recordings of sessions and transcripts as well as through clinical super-vision. Competence can thereby be assessed through adherence to the manual.

This means of assessing competence has many obvious limitations. To date there are only a limited number of therapies that have been manu-alized. (See for example, Strupp and Binder, 1984, for time limited psychodynamic therapy, Beck *et al.*, 1979, cognitive therapy for depres-sion.) Although manuals may be very helpful to researchers, and to allow assessors to state that the counsellor is competent to use the manualized therapy for the client group for whom it was intended, the reality for most counsellors is that they need to be competent to work with a range of clients and to be able to adapt their model to the needs of the environment they work in. There is also no guarantee that the counsellor, who is able to work perfectly within the model prescribed and adhere to all the guidelines, will be associated with a positive outcome for the client.

THE USE OF SKILLS TAXONOMIES

There are many skills taxonomies both published and unpublished that are in current usage on counsellor training courses, some of which are discussed here. In 1985 Ponterotto and Furlong published an article reviewing rating scale instruments used to evaluate counsellor effectiveness. They looked at the six most frequently used scales at that time, reviewing their validity, reliability and pragmatic utility. They commented that a popular method of assessing counsellor effectiveness has been through ratings collected from clients after counselling sessions but that little attention had been paid to the reliability properties of the instruments used. Scofield and Yoxheimer (1983) looked at all studies that had included measures of counsellor competencies in clinical situations and found that only 43 per cent included reliability data and only 12 per cent were accompanied by evidence of their validity. They were concerned that the indicators used actually measured the variables, traits, characteristics and abilities that are critical to counsellor competence. The instruments investigated included those used to evaluate 'real or simulated clinical situations made by trained observers, supervisors, and clients as well as clinical analogues and traditional written tests. Self evaluations by counsellors and therapists were not included' (p.414). The sample included 145 studies and 235 instances of measuring competencies of which 91 per cent assessed interpersonal competencies such as empathy, expertness, questioning, non verbal responses or overall effectiveness. The remaining 9 per cent concerned evaluative skills, the ability to detect suicide risk, clinical problem solving and knowledge of counselling strategies. Of the 43 per cent that were accompanied by reliability data, 81 per cent gave instances of inter-rater reliability. The others included references to specific prior evidence of reliability or made claims without evidence. This research mentioned the Barrett-Lennard Relationship Inventory (1962) which measures facilitative conditions and overall effectiveness as having made the best attempt at validation. However they criticized all the rating scales by saying that although it is not impossible that results can generalize across rating scales, there is no data to suggest that they do. Several methods are suggested for establishing construct validity of competency assessment instruments, including comparing the performance of experienced practitioners versus that of trainees or nominated superior performers against those described as average or poor. Four of the inventories referred to are described in the next section.

Inventories reviewed by Ponterotto and Furlong

1. The Barrett-Lennard Relationship Inventory (1962) was developed as part of his doctoral dissertation, sponsored by Carl Rogers, and is intended to measure the client's experience of their counsellor's response, which he claims to be the 'primary determinant of therapeutic influence' (Ponterotto and Furlong, 1985, p.606). The original 85-item inventory (which has been modified by many subsequent users) evaluated five concepts associated with person-centred counselling; 'level of regard (e.g. "He finds me dull and uninteresting" (-ve)); empathic understanding (e.g. "He appreciates exactly how the things I experience feel to me" (+ve)); congruence (e.g. "I feel

that he puts on a role or front with me" (-ve)), unconditionality (e.g. "How much he likes or dislikes me is not altered by anything that I tell him about myself" (+ve)) and willingness to be known (e.g. "He is more interested in expressing and communicating himself than in knowing and understanding me" (-ve)). Each concept was represented by 16 to 18 items on a 6 point scale' (p.606). This is an inventory that is completed by clients, hence only gives one perspective on competence, contrary to the social constructionist perspective on assessment which advocates a broader view of counsellor performance.

2. The Counsellor Rating Form (CRF) (Barak and LaCrosse, 1975) was developed to measure counsellor expertness, attractiveness and trustworthiness as dimensions of counsellor influence with the client using a social influence model. It uses polarized words such as enthusiasm–indifference. Although the CRF has been the most frequently used counsellor rating instrument, research examining the stability of CRF ratings has been inconclusive. It again uses client ratings and while it may be interesting as a research tool it would seem to be unfair to include an estimate of attractiveness in an assessment of competence for all counsellors. A shorter version of the rating scale has been developed by Corrigan and Schmidt (1983) which consists of only twelve items, four for each of the dimensions of expertness, attractiveness and trustworthiness.

3. The Linden, Stone and Shertzer (1965) Counselor Evaluation Inventory (CEI), is a 68-item client rating scale of the effectiveness of counsellors. It was designed to assess non-academic, non-intellectual variables in counsellors at a time when counsellors were too frequently assessed on academic ability. The inventory includes items clustered under three factors, counselling climate, counsellor comfort and client satisfaction. Examples of the statements included under each factor are given below:

COUNSELLING CLIMATE

I distrusted the counsellor.
The counsellor acted cold and distant.
The counsellor was very patient.
I believe the counsellor had a genuine desire to be of service to me.

COUNSELLOR COMFORT

The counsellor acted uncertain of himself.
The counsellor gave the impression of 'feeling at ease'.

In opening our conversations the counsellor was relaxed and at ease.

CLIENT SATISFACTION

The counsellor helped me to see how taking tests would be helpful to me.
The counsellor's discussion of test results was helpful to me.
Other students could be helped by talking to the counsellor.

As can be seen from the sample items, this scale is now out of date and would not be applicable to counselling trainees in general in Britain, because tests are not widely used in a counselling context.

4. The Counsellor Effectiveness Scale (Ivey and Authier, 1978) was developed primarily for use in micro-skills training research, the model of counselling training following a person-centred approach pioneered by Ivey and Authier. It is another scale that measures client attitudes towards the counsellor. It has been shown to be a useful instrument to evaluate counsellors before and after micro-skills training sessions, although it has been found to be highly reactive to changes in the client's environment and hence not widely applicable. It uses polarized adjectives that describe counsellor behaviour or attitudes that are rated on a seven-point scale. Examples are: sensitive versus insensitive, relevant versus irrelevant, nervous versus calm.

THE COUNSELLING SELF ESTIMATE INVENTORY

Mention has been made earlier of the importance of counsellors being able to evaluate their own competence and performance as an important aspect of their continuing professional development. The Counselling Self Estimate Inventory (Larson *et al.*, 1992) is, as the name implies, an instrument to be used by counsellors to assess their own competence. The inventory is organized in five sections to reflect the counsellor's confidence in using micro-skills, attending to process, dealing with difficult client behaviours, their cultural competence and awareness of values. It is scored on a six-point scale for each item.

The micro-skills section includes statements of confidence in the way that interpretations are made, the way that clients are confronted, clarity of communication as well as the use of assessment skills. The process section includes statements that ask counsellors to reflect on their ability to attend to the development of the counselling relationship and the process of change.

The difficult client behaviours section includes statements that invite counsellors to reflect on their ability to work with a range of problems, particularly working with clients who do not seem to be motivated or committed to counselling. The cultural competence section includes statements that invite the counsellor to think about their effectiveness with clients of a different social class or their competence in working with culturally different clients. Finally the awareness of values section invites reflection on the counsellor's awareness of their own personal values and beliefs. It includes statements about giving advice, being non judgemental, allowing personal difficulties in the counsellor's private life to impinge on the counselling relationship and communicating on an intellectual level.

This inventory has been put to the test in several studies (Larson *et al.*, 1992) and items have been found to be internally consistent and stable over time (p. 105).

> Validity estimates have shown that the instrument is (a) positively related to counselor performance, self concept, problem solving appraisal performance, expectations and class satisfaction;
> (b) negatively related to state and trait anxiety; (c) minimally related to aptitude, achievement, personality type, and defensiveness; and
> (d) sensitive to change over the course of a training programme and across different levels of counsellors.

The inventory has been designed to focus on generic competencies that are not tied to any particular theoretical orientation.

This inventory could be used on a course that places significant emphasis on self assessment as both formative and summative assessment. It could be useful on any course as an instrument to use in self, peer and tutor led appraisals. Each item could generate considerable self reflection and discussion. It may not be helpful to use this inventory as a final summative assessment of competence. Most students will be aware of how they should score the items to produce a favourable result for themselves. Most will be aware of the behaviour expected from them, even if they find it difficult to conform to what is expected. For example, 'I am afraid that I may not be able to effectively relate to someone of lower socioeconomic status than me.'

If the self assessment exercise were to be viewed as a final examination, a candidate would be very unlikely to agree with that statement even if they thought that it might be true of themselves. On the other hand, judgement of how a person thinks they will behave in a certain situation partly determines how they will behave. Self efficacy has been described by Bandura (1984, p.233) as a 'generative capability in which multiple subskills must be flexibly orchestrated in dealing with continuously changing realities, often containing ambiguous, unpredictable and stressful elements' and is based on the notion that people's sense of what they know how to do and what they actually do being similar. The inventory could prove to be a valuable tool.

The competent counsellor scale

The competent counsellor scale has been developed by Crouch (1992) to be used in the training of counsellors. He has recently updated it and it now underpins nationally available qualifications offered by CPCAB (Counselling and Psychotherapy Central Awarding Body, Glastonbury). It is intended to be generic, hence being relevant to all models of counselling. The version reproduced here does not include any form of rating scale and is to be used by staff, students and peers to monitor competence development. Crouch would like to see the accreditation of counsellors devolved to trainers and supervisors and suggests that this instrument could be used as an assessment tool in that process. Competency statements such as these can be constructively used in an appraisal interview, but considerable work would need to be done to test validity and reliability before such an instrument could be used more widely. The 33-competency statements are given below. It is interesting to note the difference between these competency statements and those given in Chapter 4.

Counsellor Awareness

Empathic awareness and skills to explore with clients their problems and their worlds.

Awareness and skills in supporting and challenging clients appropriately.

Awareness and skills in forming, sustaining and ending relationships with clients.

Awareness and skills in working therapeutically with the client's personal history.

Awareness and skills in working therapeutically with the client's patterns of social relating.

Intuitive and creative awareness necessary for the deep reflection of patterns, connections and themes.

Facility with a range of intervention, methods and techniques.

On-going awareness of the client-counsellor relationship.

Awareness of working with the client's internal and external boundaries.

Personal Work

Has begun to explore him/herself through self-disclosure and being present with others in a genuine way.

Has developed a ground of trust in self and other, sufficient to both support and challenge and be supported and challenged.

Has worked through primary personal issues of beginning, sustaining and ending relationships.

Has explored his/her personal history in both self-supportive and challenging ways.

Has explored his/her personal patterns of relating and sexuality in both self-supportive and challenging ways.

Has honestly examined his/her 'bad' and 'dark' side as well as that which is more acceptable and related this to the desire to counsel others.

Has worked on the developmental origins of his/her personal issues and patterns such that similar issues are not avoided and/or acted out in work with clients.

Has worked on personal relationship issues (e.g. rejection by others) such that these interpersonal experiences are not avoided and/or acted out in work with clients.

Has explored, supported and challenged his/her personal internal boundaries and ways of creating external boundaries.

Theoretical Understanding

Has explored the nature, practise and objectives of counselling.

Has examined ways of working with a broad selection of client groups and client problems.

Has examined ethical and practice issues including the need for supervision, support and on-going monitoring of professional competence.

Has explored theories of human development and their relevance to counselling.

Has explored theories of human relating, sexuality and group life as they relate to counselling.

Has explored theories of human nature and their implications for counselling practice.

Has explored theories of the development of client problems.

Has explored theories of the client-counsellor relationship.

Has examined theories of psychopathology and explored the professional boundaries of counselling.

Casework Skills

Skills of confidential record keeping and presentation of client work in supervision.

Skills in the application of learning within the training group to work with clients.

Skills in the effective presentation of his/her awareness, skills and understandings through case studies.

Skills in identifying and creating necessary support and supervision for both personal and client needs.

Skills in working within organisational and inter-agency contexts.

Skills in developing referral contacts and presenting his/her services to appropriate bodies.

(Reproduced with permission from Dr A Crouch, CPCAB, 3 Meadow View, Glastonbury, Somerset BA6 8DY

In summary there are rating scales or skills taxonomies to be consulted and considered that might inform some element of competence assessment but nothing yet exists that can be deemed to be valid in all circumstances, reliable or comprehensive. The problem of inter-rater agreement is ever present even if the raters happen to be clients (Liston *et al.*, 1981). The NVQ competencies discussed later in Chapter 8 are comprehensive but their reliability is yet to be put to the test.

THE USE OF AUDIO OR VIDEO TAPES IN THE ASSESSMENT OF COUNSELLOR COMPETENCE

Some of the rating scales that have been mentioned above could be used in conjunction with the review of an audio or video tape made of a real or role played counselling session. There is considerable controversy around the use of taped sessions with real clients as part of counsellor training. Ethical issues have to be carefully considered before the decision to use this method is made. (See Horton and Bayne, 1994). There are advantages and disadvantages for both client, counsellor and trainers. For the counsellor it may be anxiety provoking to open their work for scrutiny by a supervisor or trainer which may in turn affect their performance, although Bowman and Roberts (1979) did not find this to be the case. On the other hand the opportunity to listen to and reflect on their work together with detailed feedback from others can be the most powerful learning experience. For the client, while there may be some discomfort initially at having their session recorded and some anxiety about how the recording will be used, these fears can be allayed if the process of recording is introduced in a way that empowers them. For example they should be told exactly how the recording will be used, who will listen to it and what will happen to the tape before any recording takes place. It should be explained that they can stop the tape at any time and refuse consent for any part of it to be used elsewhere. Their consent must be gained and recorded. The advantage for the client is that the counsellor gives considerably more time and attention to the client's concerns and the counselling process which will serve to enhance their understanding and competence.

Kagan (1963) developed a method of training counsellors called Interpersonal Process Recall (IPR), that included tape recording as an essential element. Sessions are reviewed soon after they are taped to enquire into the interaction and process in-depth. This process could form part of a live assessment of a counsellor, rated by an observer but it is of more value as a tool for training than for assessing skill. For the trainer one disadvantage of working with taped sessions is that they can be very time consuming but this is outweighed by the advantage of hearing and perhaps seeing the counsellor at work. Close supervision of counselling work without tapes is essential and an excellent learning medium but even more can be gained through the session captured on tape (Aveline, 1992). Key moments on the tape can be replayed for further reflection. Interventions can be considered and refined and bad habits or technical errors can be illuminated.

SAMPLE MARKING SCHEME FOR TAPED ASSIGNMENT

1. Name of student ....
2. Name of marker ....
3. Date...

The tape

1.	Appropriate beginning and ending.	1.2.3.4.5.6.7.8.9.10
2.	Pace/Use of silence.	1.2.3.4.5.6.7.8.9.10
3.	Climate of understanding.	1.2.3.4.5.6.7.8.9.10
4.	Clarity of communication/interaction.	1.2.3.4.5.6.7.8.9.10
5.	Therapeutic alliance.	1.2.3.4.5.6.7.8.9.10
6.	Using questions appropriately.	1.2.3.4.5.6.7.8.9.10
7.	Using the transference.	1.2.3.4.5.6.7.8.9.10
8.	Using countertransference to inform interpretations.	1.2.3.4.5.6.7.8.9.10
9.	Use of metaphor, linking past and present.	1.2.3.4.5.6.7.8.9.10
10.	Allowing emotional discomfort.	1.2.3.4.5.6.7.8.9.10
11.	Appropriate level of challenge and confrontation.	1.2.3.4.5.6.7.8.9.10

Total   A   ....

DEDUCT for the following

1.	Being judgemental.	0.1.2.3.4.5.6.7.8.9.10
2.	Inappropriate self revelation.	0.1.2.3.4.5.6.7.8.9.10
3.	Inappropriate advice giving.	0.1.2.3.4.5.6.7.8.9.10
4.	Inappropriate use of technique.	0.1.2.3.4.5.6.7.8.9.10
5.	Other.	0.1.2.3.4.5.6.7.8.9.10

Total   B   ....

Deduct Total B from Total A   Final Total   ....

Process report

1.	Introduction and formulation.	1.2.3.4.5.6.7.8.9.10
2.	Significance of the timing of the session w.r.t. breaks, endings, etc.	1.2.3.4.5.6.7.8.9.10
3.	Use of process rather than content comments.	1.2.3.4.5.6.7.8.9.10

4. Links with theoretical understanding.   1.2.3.4.5.6.7.8.9.10
5. Recognition of strengths.   1.2.3.4.5.6.7.8.9.10
6. Recognition of weaknesses.   1.2.3.4.5.6.7.8.9.10
7. Awareness and use of transference.   1.2.3.4.5.6.7.8.9.10
8. Awareness and use of countertransference.   1.2.3.4.5.6.7.8.9.10
9. Awareness of unconscious communication.   1.2.3.4.5.6.7.8.9.10
10. Conceptualization of client material (realistic   1.2.3.4.5.6.7.8.9.10
    future plan).
11. Evidence of learning from the exercise.   1.2.3.4.5.6.7.8.9.10
12. Report presentation.   1.2.3.4.5.6.7.8.9.10

                                      Total   ....

The two scores for the tape and process report need to be viewed together. The average score does not have to be taken, but should be used as a guideline. Students must *pass* in both sections.

Figure 5.1 *Sample marking scheme for taped assignment*

Tape recorded sessions can be used as part of the assessment of formative development. It would be wrong to expect a trainee to present a taped session for a final assessment unless they were familiar with the process. Taped sessions are time consuming to listen to, but they provide a powerful learning medium. Clients are all different and a sample of work with more than one client gives a broader picture of the counsellor's capabilities. If used for summative assessment, criteria with which to assess tapes will need to be produced and tested for inter-rater reliability. Whether assessed by self, peers, tutors, supervisors or external examiners a scale will be needed for each element of the criteria used, if only at the minimal level of pass/fail. In this instance an overall pass mark would have to reflect a certain number of passes awarded for individual items. As an example Figure 5.1 shows the criteria used for the assessment of audio tapes produced as part of competence assessment for a psychodynamic course. These tapes are accompanied by a transcript and process recording, which includes the student's comments on the process of the therapy, their thoughts and feelings, transference and countertransference, awareness of mistakes, commentary on the underlying issues that affect the client's communication, etc.

McLeod (1992) has commented on the lack of research related to tape recorded sessions used in assessment and is concerned about the lack of evidence on the affect of tape recording on counsellor performance or client behaviour. He quotes Mintz and Luborsky (1971) who have produced some evidence that assessment of whole sessions is more valid than choosing short sections and Safinofsky (1979) who described a method of using video with a 'standard' client at the beginning and end of training to assess progress and development as a result of training. The issue of using a 'standard' client, one who is trained to present the same concerns in a similar way to a succession of counsellors or indeed the use of role play clients for assessment purposes is discussed in the next section.

ROLE PLAY OR REAL CLIENTS USED IN ASSESSMENT EXERCISES

Most of the rating scales described above are intended for use with real clients in counselling sessions, and many rely on a rating from the client. There are however ethical constraints in using work with real clients for assessment purposes and for this and other reasons, role play or simulated 'standard' client methods are sometimes used. Real clients are all different and present varying degrees of difficulty and complexity. Some clients are open to change and gratify counsellors by making rapid progress and others make less movement. Assessing competence using measures of outcome with clients is considered to be unreliable by Shaw and Dobson (1988) who say that even when clients are conveniently long-term, it is impossible to demonstrate development in counsellor competence by comparing severity of client symptoms at the beginning and later on in therapy because too many factors may have influenced the client's life.

In some training programmes the variability of patient difficulty is controlled by using interviews with standard cases that are simulated by actors or actresses (Mumford, *et al.*, 1987; Sharpley, *et al.*, 1994). A typical client is trained to present the same genuine concern for all interviews with trainee counsellors. It is then possible to compare the performance of trainees with each other or to repeat the same exercise after a period of training to compare pre- and post-training experiences. Sharpley *et al.* (1994) concluded 'that assessment of counsellor behaviour in terms of its impact upon the client's immediate experience of rapport can be satisfactorily performed via the standardised client procedure' (p.81).

A useful study by Gallagher and Hargie (1989) investigated the validity of role play as a procedure for counsellor skill assessment. They analysed video recordings of twelve counsellors performing in both real and simulated counselling sessions and comparison of counsellor performance between the two conditions revealed little difference. The implication from this study is that, despite tendencies reported in social skills research for simulated sessions to produce superior performance (Higgins *et al.*, 1983) and the suggestion that the lack of consequences in a role play situation would result in a more skilled performance, role play can be a valid and effective medium of assessing counsellor competence.

EXAMINATIONS AND TESTS

The assessment of competence has traditionally be carried out through the use of examinations or tests, seen or unseen. 'Pigs are not fattened by being weighed, as critics of assessment are quick to point out. Why invest time, thought and money in assessing students thoroughly when it would be better to concentrate on the business of teaching?' (Brown and Knight, 1994, p.11). Examinations are limiting in some respects particularly when they are assessed by tutors and provide no opportunity for reflection on the content. On the other hand every new client that a counsellor sees provides a new challenge to understanding and might be considered an unseen examination, an unknown and unrehearsed performance is required. None the less examinations make people anxious and a formal environment for testing may not be conducive to a good performance.

What might an examination for counsellors seek to measure? There will be a difference between a written and a verbal or practical test. For example a counselling session with a trained client could be set up under examination conditions with a video or audio tape recorder present and a subsequent evaluation of the session could be made. A written test may seek to question knowledge of theory, ethics, assessment criteria or ability to think about case material. The use of examinations encourages students to revise, read and perhaps try to memorize facts in order to perform well, when in fact the skill they really need to perform well as counsellors is to use a synthesis of all they have learned in an integrated and non-intellectual manner. 'It appears widely accepted that examinations can only address dimensions of cognitive skill and knowledge within counsellor competence rather than interpersonal skills which are required in interaction with clients' (McLeod, 1993, p.366).

Chevron and Rounsaville (1983) compared a multiple choice examination with other forms of assessment of counsellor competence and found it was unfavourable compared to other methods, particularly ratings from clients. Clinical psychology training in Britain has relied on the use of examinations for assessment purpose (Glasgow and Eisenberg, 1987) although questions are now being raised about their appropriateness. 'Why do we insist on trainees trying to acquire a wide knowledge base which we cannot test, they do not use and is impossible to learn? Surely we need to determine whether trainees know how to use the body of psychological literature in a critical and constructive manner to further their understanding of clinical problems' (p.54).

While current trends in higher education are towards adopting creative modes of assessment that eschew formal examinations (Habeshaw, Gibbs, and Habeshaw, 1993), one course has recently introduced an examination into its portfolio of assessment exercises. The examination relates to a module on professional ethics and clinical decision making. The examination presents students with a range of client material in written, audio and video format, in response to which they are required to identify defence mechanisms, make clinical assessments or discuss ethical dilemmas. Although the anxiety about being tested has been unwelcome, in some ways the examination set up mirrors the clinical setting in which counsellors have to think on their feet and make important decisions without the benefit of immediate consultation. It is therefore a reasonable measure of clinical competence with respect to assessment and students also benefit from a chance to learn from their mistakes.

ESSAYS AND CASE STUDIES

It is unlikely that many counselling training courses exist that do not use essays and written case studies as part of the assessment process. For either, the nature of the assignment will determine how much the exercise will evaluate competence. For example if students are asked to write a case study of a client they have worked with it would be relatively easy for them to relate the client's story which would tell the reader nothing about the counsellor. On the other hand if the instructions for the assignment require the counsellor to comment on the process of sessions, critical aspects of the counsellor-client relationship, helpful and unhelpful interventions, progress of the therapy, assessment of client difficulties, prognosis for future sessions, etc., then the work may have a valuable contribution to make to an assessment of competence. Similarly topics prescribed for essays may reveal much about the way a student is able to link theory and practice, or how they process complex ideas, although there is little evidence to suggest that academic ability is correlated with clinical competence (Beutler *et al.*, 1986). The question is also raised here about whether writing ability itself should be part of the assessment in counsellor training. Can someone be a good clinician but lack good written communication skills? Given the dearth of evidence available to answer such a question, it is perhaps safe to assume that setting written assignments is based more on convenience, tradition and lack of alternatives than their actual suitability for the task of assessment of competence.

COMPUTER SIMULATIONS

Inevitably in this computer age considerable effort has been invested in using computer technology in both the training and assessment of counsellors (Phillips, 1984). At its simplest level, interactive computer programmes can be used for examination purposes. Multiple choice questions appear on the screen, students tap in their responses and the programme produces a score. More sophisticated systems have been devised using simulated client-counsellor interaction. For example the Computer Counseling Simulation (CCS) utilizes six types of questions to assess twenty skills. Sharf and Lucas (1993) conducted a trial in which counsellor responses were rated by three raters and found that counsellors with advanced training selected the correct responses more often than counsellors with less training and experience. They concluded that methods such as the CCS could be developed to measure counselling skills as well as in the evaluation of the effectiveness of training. McLeod (1993) quotes the work of Berven and Scofield (1980) who summarized the use of computer simulations in the evaluation of competence as being related to interviewing skill and case management. Phillips (1984) has considered the contributions and limitations in the use of computers in counsellor training and concluded that they have much to contribute including 'information storage and retrieval, programmed instruction, research and evaluation, simulations and experimental modelling of psychological intervention' (p.191). However she challenges the computing fraternity to develop ways to 'translate current understanding of human functioning and intervention into terms that are compatible with the computer' (p.191) which will require the collaboration of other professionals. Birtle and Buckingham (1995) are pioneers in this field, an alliance between a psychotherapist and a computing academic successfully working on a cognitive model of assessment for psychotherapy using a computing interface. Perhaps their next project could be assessment of suitability for counselling training and, ultimately, for the award of a licence to practise.

LEARNING JOURNALS AND DIARIES

The last assessment tool that must be included in this overview of methods and means is the use of learning statements, personal diaries or journals and/or learning contracts. Many courses incorporate a learning journal as part of the self directed and self assessed learning process that characterizes counselling training but in only some cases are they used in summative assessment. They are regularly used in the assessment of personal development and hence will be discussed in depth in the next chapter.

SIX

Assessing personal development

The reasons for undertaking counsellor training are many and varied. Personal development may be a conscious objective of trainees. They may expect to gain self knowledge and understanding that will lead to enhanced self confidence, an inevitable by-product of being in a learning environment in which new ideas are presented and discussed and habitual attitudes and ways of relating to others are challenged. A step in any new direction whether it be to take a flower arranging course or to ride in a hot air balloon will contribute to personal development of an individual, although specific attention is not always paid to the impact on self esteem or self awareness as a result of such events.

In counsellor training, personal development is not only expected it is also required. Personal development can be defined in terms of self awareness and change. All learning opportunities that are embraced and used will produce change if only in knowledge base. More profoundly, education and training will lead to shifts in attitudes, perception and response modes. If no such changes occur, then either the training is at fault and no significant contact is made between teacher and taught or the trainee does not allow themselves to be open to learning from their experience. For counsellors every encounter with a client can be equated with a learning experience. The client is unknown and seeks to be understood. The counsellor's task is to learn about the client, taking in their communication with all their senses. If counsellors defend themselves against learning, against allowing themselves to engage in an uncharted, unpredictable learning experience with their clients, then they cannot help them.

An essential requirement of a counsellor is that they are open to learning about themselves and others and flexible and open enough to be able to be affected and change. Personal development is not only desirable of counsellors in training but a requirement. It is not possible to quantify how much trainees should change or indeed to generalize about how, but there must be some evidence throughout and at the end of training that significant shifts have occurred. Counsellor training must therefore incorporate some element of assessment of personal development although the format of such an assessment will vary widely depending on the orientation of the course and the inclinations of the assessors.

DESIGNING AN ASSESSMENT SCHEME THAT INCLUDES PERSONAL DEVELOPMENT

Personal or self development, personal growth or self awareness are often stated objectives of counselling course students, but at the same time may be quite threatening concepts. Hence introducing the notion of assessment of personal development will create anxiety in students and whenever possible such assessment should be part of a course from the beginning. As with other elements of a course, criteria for assessment should be clearly detailed in any pre-course information so that students know it exists. Assessing personal development can be construed as a judgemental activity with a subjective component. It is one thing to be judged on one's essay writing or even counselling skills but when an assessment touches on even more personal issues the stakes are higher and the potential for pain and conflict increase.

PERSONAL DEVELOPMENT OPPORTUNITIES

Counselling courses are usually rich in opportunities for self development, through seminars and discussions, case work and supervision, personal therapy or group experiences, reading and research, tutorials and interaction with other students. One course has even included an outward-bound-type outdoor experience into the curriculum which had a powerful effect on the participants (Goldie, 1995). Many courses require students to keep a journal, diary or log throughout the course with the aim of encouraging the monitoring of experience and change.

Pates and Knasel (1989) have described the use of a learning record as a mechanism for the assessment of a student's progress on an RSA counselling training course. The RSA guidelines for successful completion of the course state (RSA, 1984):

Assessment should be carried out by the use of an individual 'Learning Record'. The Learning Record should identify the key learning experiences gathered by the participant which, subject to discussion between participants and between participant and tutor, will outline agreed progress made and steps taken. Each discussion should be recorded in the journal and accredited by the tutor.

The learning record is owned by the people keeping it and forms the basis for tutorial sessions, although control is retained by the writer. It should incorporate evidence of learning in a variety of forms, such as statements about self, ideas, reflections, observations, statements from peers and tutors as well as score sheets from exercises or instruments that form part of the course. It is concluded at the end of the course by a Learning Record Statement, a summary of experience and development. 'Reflective learning is a natural process used spontaneously by many people. Once aware of the process, greater conscious control will stimulate more effective control' (Boyd and Fales, 1983, p.98).

Pates and Knasel (1989) analysed learning records kept by students participating on their courses and gained useful feedback about the course itself, the way the record was used as a vehicle for reflection as well as different approaches to compiling it. They noted that 'the course is a period of learning through reflection which draws on a variety of experience that will be different for each participant: essentially, the learning is derived from the outcomes of situations experienced during the time span of the course, rather than inputs per se.' The range of reflection included in the record spanned performance and relationships at work, attitudes to other people, course experiences including lectures, projects, group work, tutorials, relationships with other course members and personal crises that occurred during the period of study.

Four different approaches to the learning record were noted. Some students kept a diary, a chronological record of events and experiences on the course and outside, with a summative statement at the end. Others created a structured learning analysis starting with a list of objectives, thoughts about how they could be achieved and finally notes on if and how they had been met. Such an analysis could be accompanied by a progress diary. A variation on the structured learning analysis was an objective-based record, which started in a similar way with a list of objectives and was followed by a detailed account of how work on each objective in turn had been approached through the vehicle of the course. Finally other students chose to create a course input-based learning record, which included a set of diary entries organized around each element of the course, such as lectures, tutorials, etc. If a system of student-centred learning is to have credibility it is important that students have some flexibility to create the learning record in their own way, however they may need help and guidance to get started and encouragement to focus on their experience and to record it on paper.

Work on a learning record must start at the beginning of a course with tutors giving substantial time to explain what is required and for students to explore ways and means of bringing the impact of experiences to their conscious awareness and recording it. Students will need to set individual learning objectives for themselves to which they can add others as more insight highlights new issues that they were unaware of at the start. Having started the project, the continuity of the record needs to be stressed, so that subtle changes can be recorded as well as major events, which are easier to remember when recalled at a later date. This can be best achieved by the arrangement of regular tutorials and peer group meetings in which the learning record can be discussed. Dates and times of discussion sessions should also be recorded. There are confidentiality implications which must be carefully negotiated. Students will be encouraged to share as much as possible with their tutors and peers and the learning record is a document that is subject to assessment, hence they may only feel able to include in it that which they are comfortable about being seen. Some may choose to keep an additional diary that records their more intimate thoughts that can then be censored before being incorporated into the main document. The final summative statement marks the end of the course and may include reference to the impact of the ending process.

While Pates and Knasel describe the learning record in great detail and extol its virtues, they do not say anything about what is and what is not acceptable, the implication being that all students complete the work in a satisfactory manner and gain from it. They are writing about a Certificate in Counselling skills, a course which does not lead to a professional qualification as a counsellor but nevertheless some criteria for acceptable completion of the learning record must surely exist. It may be that students make an assessment of the documents and decide amongst themselves about the criteria for acceptability, but this seems a little unfair if such criteria are only developed when the course is almost at an end. It is more likely that the course staff have a notion of what is acceptable and what is not but that might be difficult to put into words. The questions are raised, What if a student shows little evidence of either personal or skills development? What if it is evident that the record has not been kept throughout the course but that a last minute retrospective commentary has been compiled? What if a student feels that they have learned a great deal about themselves and have gained from the experience of the course but still cannot use counselling skills effectively? What if both peers and tutors are aware of an area of difficulty that a student has that they cannot acknowledge and hence cannot confront? Whereas an essay can be rewritten or a video taped counselling session repeated, a learning record can only relate to the course experience and can only be repeated if the student takes on another course to record. Tutors sometimes have to make the painful and difficult decision to tell a student that they are unsuitable to be counsellors. It is often put in terms of more personal development being needed. Unfortunately, it is usually the students who defend themselves against hearing any negative or critical feedback and hence cannot use it constructively to make changes, who are the most convinced that they are competent and the most angry when they fail, but more of this in Chapter 7.

Learning journals are regularly used on counselling courses to monitor and sometimes assess personal development. Connor (1994) describes the use made of learning journals as an essential element of her Diploma in Counselling at York, College of Ripon and York, St John, particularly in assessing the core of her training model (see Chapter 2) described as intra-personal and interpersonal development. She says (p.168):

> Learning objectives for intra-personal development include: understanding and appreciation of self; awareness of and utilisation of personal strengths and assets; awareness of blind spots, blocks and vulnerabilities; identification of areas to work on in personal counselling and experiential appreciation of the significance of developmental stages in personal development. Learning objectives for interpersonal development include an understanding of areas of strength and areas for development in a range of interactions; gaining confidence in appropriate self sharing; developing the skills of giving and receiving feedback; facilitating growth in self and others through active participation in personal learning development groups; developing helping relationships with clients; continuously reflecting upon successes and setbacks; developing the internal supervisor.

She mentions further aims and objectives that can be monitored through the journal in Stage 1 of her course model, assessing attitudes and values. These learning objectives include: 'awareness of personal assumptions and beliefs; exploration and clarification of values and attitudes' (p.172).

These are clearly pre-set learning objectives that apply to all students. Each student will have their individual starting point and may reach varying end points, but evidence of progress within each objective is required. The challenge is to determine how such achievements can be recognized and who should make the judgement about whether the progress is satisfactory. Connor suggests that each of these objectives can be made specific for each student, who may then be required to collect both quantitative and qualitative evidence that goals have been kept in sight if not always totally met. She describes the trainee as being at the heart of the assessment process with the trainer involved at a second level monitoring the use of the learning journal as a tool for reflection, understanding and subsequent change. She also specifies the criteria for assessing learning journals (p.169):

> Based on three core objectives:
>
> 1. That learning objectives have been regularly set and reflected upon;
> 2. That all aspects of learning on the counselling course, including unstructured learning and client work, are included;

3. That there is evidence of movement as a result of reflection upon learning.

She has met the criticism made of Pates and Knasel by clearly identifying what is needed to meet the course requirements (p.170):

1. Regular weekly entries of a minimum of one side of A4 paper.
2. Ongoing learning objectives specified, evaluated and reflected upon.
3. Clear legible presentation.
4. Links made with other course documents, e.g. essays, supervised counselling practice file, notes on reading.
5. Evidence of reflection on learning in all parts of the course: theory and workshop sessions, training group, group supervision, experiential group, review partner, practice in the work setting and individual supervision.
    Reflections where appropriate may also be included on learning from individual counselling or therapy and from significant life events and experiences.
6. Evidence of movement, learning and insight with regard to self and others.
7. Summary sheets at the end of each term.
8. Personal Development Profile of approximately 1,500 words at the end of each year.

These guidelines give students a clear indication of the quantity and content that is expected. The subjective nature of assessing such work is not addressed. While a student may think that they have provided evidence of change, others may still see huge gaps in their development that throws their competence into question. Who makes the judgement as to whether the student has achieved the aims and objectives satisfactorily and what must that student do if this has not happened?

A novel approach to the assessment of self development is currently being pioneered by the MA Counselling Course at the University of Birmingham. It is based on a system of self and peer appraisal. The course often has a profound impact on students, both because of the theoretical material presented and the intense learning experience in academic, clinical and personal spheres and considerable change is reported both verbally and written in summative statements at the end of each year. However tutors were concerned that while some students, whose lack of personal development impedes their potential for work with clients, are forced to face difficult issues when they fail clinical or other assignments, others manage to cover up their prejudices, blind spots or other negative qualities sufficiently to meet the formal demands of the course. Tutors may feel concerned about an individual, offer feedback and support, but it is not necessarily taken seriously or acted upon. Hence the decision was taken to pilot a scheme that placed personal development squarely in the middle of the assessment process.

Students are required to keep a journal throughout the course although the content remains private. They are however required to engage in a self and peer assessment exercise twice each year of a two-year course. They are given a series of sheets to complete that asks them to think about the worst criticism and qualities valued and admired that might be seen by members of the course community. Comments are made under the headings of communication, self image, sensitivity, openness to self reflection, willingness to adopt a different viewpoint-broad perspectives and personal prejudices. Under each heading students are required to write what they think of themselves and what they imagine others, in particular a course peer, a member of their personal development group, a course tutor and a client, think of them. The sheets are completed by each individual and are then taken for discussion to a peer appraisal group. As a result of that discussion the amended sheets are discussed with personal tutors, who are core members of the staff team. The appraisal sheets may then be amended again until both parties are satisfied with the content. At this point tutor and student sign the sheets, which are included in the personal development portfolio that has to be submitted at the end of the course. It is hoped that this process will provide a stimulating learning experience, as well as being a vehicle for confronting sensitive personal issues with students when necessary. The pilot scheme will be evaluated at the end of a two-year cycle and modified or abandoned as deemed to be appropriate.

Finally, personal development may be directly or indirectly assessed through assignments that are set throughout a course. Essays can include an element of self exploration, written case studies can reveal a lot about the way a student approaches their clients and tape or video recorded counselling sessions can highlight personal development issues that require attention. Such issues may be the reason that an assignment cannot be passed. Brief examples of how personal development difficulties are demonstrated include the following.

Samual presented his taped recorded counselling session for assessment. At the beginning of it he wrote, 'This work may have been influenced by the fact that just before the session I had received a message that my mother had been rushed to hospital and was critically ill'. The assignment was failed because it demonstrated his lack of awareness of his own needs, as well as contravening the BAC Code of Ethics that requires counsellors to abstain from seeing clients when they are emotionally stressed themselves (BAC, 1990).

In an essay on countertransference Justine gave several examples of her response to clients and how the countertransference was used. Towards the end of the essay she described as countertransference the negative feelings she had towards male clients. She stated clearly that she was terrified of men and would only see men as clients if she was pushed to do so.

PERSONAL THERAPY AND GROUP WORK

Personal development can occur through any experiences that people have but the label is most readily given to experiences that are contrived to promote personal growth such as personal therapy and development group experiences. Most professional counselling training courses require students to engage in one or other of these activities. There is some debate about whether personal therapy should be a course requirement. Some say that students should choose to have therapy when they think that it would be appropriate and they feel ready and able to use it. Forcing people to have therapy when they have not experienced the need for themselves can lead to a less than satisfactory experience for both student and therapist. Requirements tend to be quite specific, for example, a minimum of thirty hours, which for one person could be a rich, fulfilling and illuminating experience and for another could feel like a waste of time and money. Being forced or required to have therapy can be a bit like being force fed without feeling hungry. Personal therapy should not be the only way in which provision is made for self development on a course. The lack of clarity in the counselling profession about the need for personal therapy is reflected in the reluctance to include therapists in the assessment process. Sometimes therapists are asked to provide an attendance statement but are not asked to comment on the suitability of their client to be a counsellor.

By its very nature, therapy is a private activity during which the client or trainee has some control over the issues raised. It is possible that an individual in therapy could ignore personal traits, values or beliefs that others may be aware of and find offensive or antithetic to some groups of people. Such blind spots are unlikely to escape attention in development or self awareness groups, a regular feature of many courses. However there is not a consensus of opinion that therapy groups should be a compulsory part of a training experience and the assessment of students' performance in such a group is also controversial. A well-trained group facilitator will be in an ideal position to comment on the way someone interacts with others, how open they are to feedback, how they manage feedback and how clear they are in communicating with others. However it is thought that adding an assessment dimension to a group experience would be too inhibiting for the participants. The group invites openness and honesty as an essential ingredient. Subjecting one's most vulnerable self, potentially unacceptable thoughts and feelings to someone who may hold a crucial pass/fail key, poses a dilemma. How will self disclosure be judged? Are some things just too awful to be accepted in the realm of courage and bravery, even if the latter two qualities are formally described as being highly valued by tutors.

Person-centred courses tend to use core staff to facilitate groups. In this case the staff will inevitably have a role in assessment. The rationale offered in this instance is that the responsibility for assessment is shared broadly amongst staff and peers as well as including substantial self assessment. (See Dryden, Horton and Mearns, 1995). On the other hand psychodynamic courses usually use an external facilitator who does not meet the students in any other role. Confidentiality of the group is an important requirement, with responsibility for the process of the group contained within the group. The facilitator cannot express their opinion about individual group members without breaking confidentiality in other than extreme circumstances (e.g. potential harm to self or others), but the result seems to be that the group takes on the responsibility for confronting unacceptable behaviour, attitudes or beliefs within the group. Consequences of this can be far-reaching. Some people make important and noticeable changes which become apparent in other course arenas, and occasionally someone drops out of the course.

Taking the decision to terminate counselling training can be an important if traumatic milestone in a person's life, and can be seen as the result of valid and brave self assessment. Despite the best of selection procedures it is impossible to know exactly what impact a training course will have on individuals. A candidate may seem highly self assured and self aware at interview but find the stimulus of lectures on human development, the pressure of colleagues or the resurrection of old doubts and fears too much to handle. While support should be offered to help such a person through a crisis, the decision to withdraw should be respected. Sometimes it is a decision welcomed by course tutors, a relief from anxiety about having selected someone who may not make the grade the course demands. Problems are greater when no such decision is made and a student painfully struggles on. Students who lack self awareness and are unable to recognize their difficulties are usually a worry for staff. This is discussed further in Chapter 7.

ATTENDANCE

Course or personal development group attendance is an essential assessment criteria. Counselling is a profession that demands personal commitment. Training courses and personal development groups can be stressful and demanding. Attendance demonstrates personal organization and commitment. If a requirement to attend is not imposed on an awareness group, it can be too easy to drop out if the going gets tough. If a member can choose not to attend a group (giving the excuse as illness, work commitments, child care, etc.) they can avoid facing uncomfortable issues that may have been

raised. The group then loses its potential to effect change in its participants.

PERSONAL DEVELOPMENT ASSESSMENT THROUGH
SUPERVISION

As with most aspects of counsellor training, personal development or
enhanced self awareness will be one of the outcomes of clinical supervision.
In the process of talking about client material and exploring the relationship
between client and counsellor blind spots and areas of discomfort in the
counsellor will become evident. Clients are unpredictable in what they
might relate and issues will sometimes emerge that the counsellor has not
faced inside themselves. The awareness that is achieved through the
supervision process is sometimes enough to enable the counsellor to work
effectively thereafter with that client, but sometimes a counselling session
or personal therapy is recommended to facilitate further exploration and
development.

The supervisor will gain over a period of time a sense of the counsellor's
skills, theoretical understanding, awareness of ethical issues, insight and
sensitivity. In addition they may encounter prejudices, attitudes or values
that conflict with professional development, personality dynamics that
inhibit their ability to learn from experience, or difficulties in resisting
instant gratification of their clients. They may be aware of the counsellor's
over-identification with the distress of their clients or resistance to allowing
emotional distress, a reluctance to engage with certain issues or an inability
to take care of themselves. Hence the supervisor is well placed to comment
on the way in which trainees manage these conflicts. A trainee who is open
to exploring their relationships with clients, who takes steps to take care of
themselves and their concerns may be deemed to be more competent to
practise than another who gets stuck in denial or adopts other defensive
strategies to avoid facing their own weaknesses. Consequently a counsellor
who has perhaps had a disturbed upbringing, which has resulted in
relationship or communication difficulties, but who is aware and open to
change, might inspire more confidence in their counselling abilities than
someone who appears to be self assured and intellectually capable, but who
is unable to look at the issues that block their understanding or communication with others.

A report from clinical supervisors that places emphasis on personal
development as well as clinical work can be an invaluable assessment tool.
Supervisors must be carefully chosen and trained for the role they fulfil on
a counselling training course. If a supervision report or assessment is to
have the weight it deserves, then guidelines for assessment must be
produced to ensure that all students are judged fairly by agreed criteria.
Also supervisors will need to be selected according to criteria relevant to the

course, such as their length of experience, theoretical orientation and training. Their induction into the expectations of the course, both of students and of supervisors, particularly with respect to assessment, must be thorough. Too often students are allowed to find their own supervisors, who may be unknown to the course team, and with whom there is little or no communication. Under such circumstances it would be quite unreasonable to place great emphasis on the supervisor's report for assessment as quality control could not be guaranteed. Appendix A shows the assessment scheme used for supervision on a BAC-recognized psychodynamic counselling course. Students who do not pass this assessment cannot pass the course and are required to undertake a further counselling placement under supervision, recommended to have personal therapy or sometimes asked to withdraw.

ASSESSMENT OF ABILITY TO WORK WITH CULTURAL DIFFERENCE, DISABILITY OR SEXUAL ORIENTATION

In Chapter 2 a model of counsellor competence was outlined which included five elements, self, other, therapeutic frame, relationship and awareness of environment factors. Clearly personal development is part of all of these domains but particularly 'self' and 'environmental factors'. It is important that counsellors are competent to work with a wide range of clients, including those who are of a different cultural background or racial group, those who may have physical or in some instances mental disabilities, and those whose sexual orientation is other than that of the counsellor. Regrettably prejudice and misunderstanding towards people in these groups is not uncommon (Liddle, 1995; Rudolph, 1988; Pearce, 1994) and a vital ingredient of all counselling training is the inclusion of some awareness training which confronts students with their own attitudes and beliefs and helps to eliminate biases that they might have against such clients. Bernard and Goodyear (1992) argue that students must be encouraged to challenge the 'myth of sameness' that counselling skills are universally applicable to individuals regardless of their cultural background or other differences.

There are many ways in which trainee counsellors can be assessed on their awareness of cultural, environmental or social context issues in counselling, although such assessment may not appear under a label that identifies it as such. For example the supervision assessment instrument described above and appended later includes such elements as:

- awareness and ability to work with racial differences
- willingness to examine their own cultural heritage and explore differences between themselves and other cultural/racial, religious/sexual groups

Similarly the appraisal scheme described earlier includes reference to 'personal prejudices and willingness to adopt a different viewpoint-broad perspectives'. This provides a vehicle for prejudice or narrow mindedness to be addressed. If someone is seen as unwilling or unable to confront their prejudices, the appraisal system should provide an incentive for exploration when used as part of the formative assessment and a gatekeeping function if improvement is not made when used as a summative assessment.

Learning journals could provide a vehicle for reflection on issues of race, disability and sexual orientation, either on a voluntary basis or as part of the prescription of what such a journal should cover. Inevitably students who have the greatest difficulty with accepting others who are different to themselves are the least likely to explore such issues without being required to do so. Similarly it could be put on the agenda of self and peer assessment exercises. Some courses include a written examination or test as part of the assessment system, in which relevant case studies can be presented for consideration. Alternatively, ethical dilemmas can be included for discussion or questions can be set that invite comment on which counselling approaches might be relevant to particular clients. Essays could be set in which students are invited to explore their own approach to working with, for example, a blind client or someone who presented suffering from AIDS.

MULTICULTURAL COUNSELLING COMPETENCIES

Considerable work has been done, particularly in the USA, to develop instruments to assess multicultural counselling competence. Inevitably these instruments include many questions on attitudes and values and hence are relevant to the discussion of personal development assessment as well as being of more general use in the assessment of skills. Ponterotto *et al.* (1994) have reviewed four instruments designed to assess multicultural counselling competence in trainees. They note that in the USA multicultural counselling is on the agenda of most training programmes although the emphasis has been on awareness of bias and prejudice and knowledge of culturally diverse values, rather than on specific skill development. All of the four scales are based on the competencies defined by Sue *et al.* (1982). Details of these instruments follow.

1. *The Cross Cultural Counseling Inventory* (CCCI) (LaFromboise, Coleman and Hernandez, 1991). This inventory is completed by an evaluator and rates twenty items on a six-point Likert scale. Competencies are organized into three general areas: cultural awareness and beliefs, cultural knowledge and flexibility in counselling skills. This instrument was the first of its kind and has received the most empirical scrutiny. It is not too long and is therefore quick and easy

to complete. Such a scale could easily be incorporated into a personal appraisal scheme or be a requirement for use in a peer review group.

2. *The Multicultural Awareness Scale Form B* (Ponterotto, Sanchez and Magids, 1991). This is a 45-item counsellor self rating scale using a seven-point Likert type format to measure cultural awareness of value biases and how these might translate into culturally insensitive counselling, knowledge of culture specific issues such as the impact of racism on clients and skills that convey awareness and knowledge in culturally sensitive interventions.

   It includes such items as:
   - I believe all clients should maintain eye contact during counseling
   - I think that clients who do not discuss intimate aspects of their lives are being resistant and defensive
   - I am aware of my limitations in cross cultural counseling and could specify them readily

   From these few examples it is obvious that this questionnaire is prone to biased answers because of social desirability but nevertheless it could be used in a peer assessment exercise or to stimulate discussion.

3. *The Multicultural Counseling Inventory* (Sodowsky *et al.*, 1994). This is a self report inventory that consists of forty-three statements asking for a response on a four-point scale. It is arranged in four subscales, multicultural counselling skills, multicultural awareness, multicultural knowledge and multicultural counselling relationship.

   Examples of statements to be rated include:
   When working with minority clients:
   - I perceive that my race causes clients to mistrust me
   - I use innovative concepts and treatment methods
   - I examine my own cultural bias
   - I tend to compare client behaviours with those of majority group members
   - I am successful at seeing 50 per cent of the clients more than once, not including intake

   As with the previous scales, this could be used to help individuals think about their values and behaviour as counsellors with minority clients or in peer review.

4. *The Multicultural Awareness Knowledge and Skills Survey* (MAKSS) (D'Andrea, Daniels and Heck, 1991) is designed 'to assess the effect of instructional strategies on students' multicultural counselling development' (Ponterotto *et al.*, 1994, p.320). The three sub-scales used for the sixty survey items include those mentioned in the previous three instruments, awareness, knowledge and skill. The

scale has been exposed to limited research to date but can discriminate between those who have been trained in multicultural counselling issues and those who have not.

These inventories may prove to be too 'American' for a British training course, but their perusal and possible adaptation could provide a useful tool in helping to ensure that counselling trainees are culturally competent.

WHO ASSESSES PERSONAL DEVELOPMENT?

Throughout this chapter reference has been made to people within the community of a counselling course that might have a role in the assessment of personal development. This has included self, peers, tutors, other course staff, supervisors, external examiners, group facilitators and personal therapists. On some courses a team approach to assessment of personal development and indeed counselling competence is taken. Such a team might be described as a professional committee. It may be made up of any of the people described above. A portfolio of assessed work, case work and reports is presented to the committee when a student wants to progress to the next stage of their training. The committee considers the student's application according to agreed criteria and makes a decision about their suitability to proceed. The deliberation will inevitably include consideration of self awareness and personal development and permission to proceed may be withheld on those grounds. This may seem quite harsh and can only operate fairly and successfully when criteria for progression are clearly stated and communicated to trainees. An appeals procedure is also required.

SUMMARY

There is quite a lot to think about when considering the assessment of personal development but it is clear that such assessment underpins everything else that is assessed during counselling training. If this is not the case then the training or the assessment scheme is seriously at fault and the competence of trainees at the end of a programme cannot be guaranteed. The next chapter looks more closely at the difficulty of managing students who raise doubts about their competence to practise as counsellors often for reasons related to personal development.

SEVEN

Assessment difficulties: ethical and professional dilemmas

INTRODUCTION

Assessment of counselling competence has been discussed from many perspectives and questions of who assesses, how they do it, when it is appropriate, what is being assessed and instruments used, have been considered. It has been established that assessment has many facets and components that make the task complex and demanding. Assessing competence can be stimulating and rewarding but it can also be exhausting and stress inducing when the process is complicated by difficulties. Students invest considerable time, money and effort into their training but they are not all successful. While clear failures are painful to deal with, the emotional and mental energy required to make a decision about a student whose competence is in doubt is considerable. The need to be fair in assessing the competence of each individual is double edged. The counselling trainer has in mind the need to be fair to the trainee but also to the clients with whom they may work. The final decision to pass a student and give them a licence to practise can weigh heavily when there are doubts about their competence. At the same time the pressure from the institution to have students successfully completing a course is hard to ignore.

EQUAL OPPORTUNITIES

Most if not all counselling training courses will want to offer equal opportunity to their students and will seek to ensure that a learning environment is created in which everyone can have access to resources, support and encouragement to reach their potential as counsellors. Courses will have overt or covert objectives that students will be expected to achieve. As has been discussed at length in Chapter 3, careful selection of trainees can help to ensure that everyone accepted on to a course has the potential to achieve the course objectives. However, there is no guarantee that everyone chosen will be able to make appropriate use of the learning experience or that everyone will develop in the way that is expected (Bradley and Post, 1991). At the time of selection (in the interest of equal opportunities or sometimes less laudable motives like filling places) the course selectors will take risks with some candidates.

Given the lack of evidence of any foolproof way to select people who will become good counsellors, there is always a chance that anyone accepted on to a course may turn out to be unsuitable for the training offered. White and Franzoni (1990) studied the mental health of 180 graduate counsellors in training and found levels of psychological disturbance to be higher than in the general population. However, sometimes the element of risk in selection is more apparent than others. Here are some examples: All of these candidates have appropriate qualifications and have completed an introductory course in counselling. They are all keen and enthusiastic to do the course and handle the interview well.

Christopher (aged thirty-seven) is working for an alcohol advisory service. He has had a rather unsettled career with lots of changes. He describes himself as a recovered alcoholic and has been completely sober for three years.

Woo Chung (aged thirty) has been a primary school teacher in Hong Kong and has come to Britain with her husband who is studying for a Phd. She is working in a local counselling agency having completed their training course. Her command of spoken English is poor. Her manner of staccato speech make her seem quite cold and detached.

Elizabeth (aged twenty-nine) is employed full time by an evangelical religious group as their welfare officer. She is totally committed to her religion and her church. When asked about her ability to set her views and values aside and work with clients who have no religious interest she is adamant that it would cause her no difficulty. She is open about her painful life experiences and her path to religious life.

Winston (aged sixty-one) is a retired social worker working in a voluntary capacity for a local counselling charity. He seems young for his years and enthusiastic to embark on a new career. His wife has died recently.

Daniel (aged thirty-four) is a Black probation officer of African-Caribbean origin. He asks many questions about how the course addresses cross-cultural issues and states his intention to work only with Black young people.

Sophie (aged twenty-seven) works in a refuge for battered women. She is extremely thin. She tells the interviewers that she had suffered from anorexia, but having been in therapy for the past five years has recovered.

Simon (aged forty) works as a telephone counsellor with blind people. He is blind himself. He is living independently and seems to manage life very well. He responds appropriately to questions in the interview but does not acknowledge any current difficulties as a result of his blindness or anticipate that any will be posed by the course.

Monica (aged thirty-one) comes to the interview dressed in long flowing robes and wearing a badge saying, 'I am lesbian and proud of it'. She makes it clear that she dislikes men and is only interested in working with women. She agrees to see men on her counselling placement as it is a course requirement.

Alistair (aged twenty-two) has a job in the local further education college as a counsellor. He had studied psychology at university and had been involved with a helpline there. He seems very young and naive but is seeing lots of clients and needs support and training.

Parminder (aged thirty-seven) is working as a volunteer counsellor in the burns unit of the local hospital. She herself has been badly burnt in an accident and her face is badly disfigured. She has been in therapy and has come to terms with her scars. She now wants to help others in a similar way.

Mohammed (aged thirty-one) is open about his Muslim fundamentalist beliefs but wants to serve his community through counselling. He has the qualifications that the course asks for but his written application is poor. In the interview he never quite answers the questions that are posed.

Geoff (aged twenty-nine) is an accountant and a volunteer in a local counselling agency. He wants to change career to become a counsellor. During the interview it is evident that he has a bad stutter. When asked about the stutter he says that he is having speech therapy and that it is at its worst when he is under stress.

The pen character sketches have been drawn to illustrate some of the dilemmas that trainers might have when selecting for a counselling training course. Any of the candidates described could turn out to be excellent students and counsellors but on the other hand there could be problems. Christopher could find the stress of training too much and start drinking again, Alistair may be too immature to cope with the training, let alone the job. Monica may turn out to be aggressively anti-men and insistent on working with women, and Elizabeth may spend all her time trying to convert fellow students, staff and clients alike to her religion. At the same time any students, however unproblematic they seemed at interview, could become a problem in an unforeseen way. The BAC Code of Ethics for Trainers states clearly that (BAC, 1995b, p.3):

A.1.3 Trainers must recognise the value and dignity of trainees with due regard to issues of origin, status, gender, age, beliefs, sexual orientation or disability. Trainers have a responsibility to be aware of their own issues of prejudice and stereo-typing, and to give particular consideration to the way in which this may be affecting the training relationship.

This statement is laudable but offers no guidance for protecting the interests of professionalism or the public, with whom trainees who complete the course may work. Indeed, the Code of Ethics makes no mention of the need to ensure that comprehensive assessment systems are devised and used by trainers and that only students who reach an agreed standard of competence are allowed to graduate from a course.

SELECTING THEMSELVES OUT

Students who find counselling training too demanding or stressful tend to select themselves out after consultation with course tutors. They may have received feedback that suggests to them that substantial changes are required or have come to their own conclusion. They may decide to drop out altogether or to take time off. This process is sometimes referred to as 'counselling out' although this phrase does not rest comfortably with the author as it suggests rather a difference sense of the word counselling than is used in this book.

ORGANIZATIONAL CONTEXT

Some institutions have more discretion to work creatively towards a satisfactory assessment of competence than others. For example, traditional educational establishments such as universities or colleges may have more rigid criteria for successful accomplishment of courses than a private counselling training agency that adheres to a counselling profession-driven standard of competence. A counselling agency may have more flexibility to develop appropriate assessment methods.

It is notoriously difficult to manage students whose failure to thrive as counselling trainees is due to personal or personality problems rather than academic concerns. Organizations have difficulty drawing up procedures for dealing with such students and even more trouble implementing them. Bradley and Post surveyed American organizations offering counselling training. Only 13 per cent reported the use of formal screening procedures to dismiss students and 29 per cent of respondents did not answer this question. 'Although most programs seem quite clear on step wise screening procedures for the typical student, they seem to be more unsure or perplexed about procedures to follow with students with mental health, drug or alcohol problems'. (Rowe *et al.*, 1975; Whitely, 1969; in Bradley and Post, 1991, p.107)

FEEDBACK DEAFNESS

A major difficulty arises when a student is unable or unwilling to hear or take on board any feedback that is perceived as negative about their performance as counsellors. Such a student's ability to learn is compromised because of their resistance to hearing anything other than praise. They may be narcissistic and find criticism, however constructive, intolerable. 'Surprise negative reactions may occur if the trainee has been denying feedback that can no longer be avoided when the evaluation is formal. However, in our experience procrastination on the part of the supervisor until "the day of judgement" has been more frequent. This behaviour often leads the trainee to feel betrayed' (Klein and Babineau, 1974, p.790). A typical scenario is that after numerous attempts to confront weaknesses and offer support, the tutor gives up and asks the student to leave. Sometimes it is made easier by failed assignments in which a lack of self awareness has been obvious. The attack (as the student perceives it) on their competence cannot be tolerated and the only possible defence is through the counter-attack of appeal. At this stage everyone loses. Staff and student are distressed by the procedure. If the student wins and returns triumphant to the course, the problem cycle starts again with less goodwill on all sides and if their appeal fails, they retaliate in other ways by appealing to a higher authority or even by taking legal action. Ingrid is an example of such a student.

Ingrid had been working as a counsellor without any formal training for ten years before she joined the course. She was of South Asian origin and worked in a counselling centre for Asian young people. During seminars she regularly challenged the speaker in a manner that suggested that she was right and they were wrong. Indeed this tendency was evident in her relationship with others. She had a habit of dismissing other people's points of view. In supervision for her casework there were difficulties. She tended to argue with the supervisor and seemed unable to take in any of the ideas or thoughts that were offered. It became clear that she had fixed traditional views of how Asian women should behave and seemed unable to allow her clients to explore their difficulties and choose solutions that did not concur with her values.

Ingrid was given feedback from her peers about how she came across to them. Her supervisor confronted her continually and eventually gave her a written assessment of her counselling work, with a copy to the course tutor because verbal feedback was ignored. Ingrid retaliated by accusing the staff of racism. Despite several meetings with her tutor, the situation did not improve and she was asked to leave. Ingrid appealed to the college authorities and to the Race Relations Board. The course staff had kept records of their meetings with her and her written and taped assignments had been poor. The college appeals board dismissed the case.

EXCLUSIONS

The Diploma course in Counselling at the University of Manchester reported having had such difficulties with several students who had attendance problem that they wrote a comprehensive procedure for removing course members who proved to be unsuitable. The procedure includes involvement by core staff members, tutors and supervisors as well as the students themselves. Students are first approached informally, to discuss the problems that have been observed by staff. A period of time is allowed to elapse before speaking to the student again if matters do not improve. The next step involves a formal meeting with two tutors at which a document detailing the concerns of the staff and the required change in behaviour is discussed and signed by all parties. The clinical supervisor's review of learning is requested with the student's permission and used in the final meeting, held if no improvement is observed. At that formal meeting with two course staff, the student is asked to leave the course. All meetings are documented and the organization authorities are kept informed throughout the process.

In order to allow some discretion in asking unsuitable students to leave a counselling course another institution includes the following in its regulations:

A candidate who fails to attain an adequate level of professional commitment and conduct, may be required by the Board . . . to withdraw from the course and the University following representation from the head of an organisation or institution in which the candidate is undertaking practical placement or teaching placement. A candidate shall not be required to withdraw without having the opportunity to make representations. (University of Birmingham Faculty Handbook, 1995, p.128)

RESEARCH INTO TRAINERS' DILEMMAS

There is little written about ethical dilemmas related to assessment in general or of students on the borderline of competence, hence the author included an investigation of how such students were managed in her research on assessment of competence. Questionnaires concerning the assessment of competence of counselling trainees were sent to 105 training establishments that advertised counselling courses at Diploma or Masters level selected from the BAC Directory of Training Courses (BAC, 1995c). Forty questionnaires were returned, although not all the questions had been answered on each form. Demographic information about the respondents is given in Table 7.1. Respondents were also asked if they would be willing to participate in an interview to discuss aspects of assessment in more detail.

Seven such interviews were conducted. Both the questionnaire and the interviews covered a range of topics including questions related to ethics and assessment difficulties that are discussed here.

Table 7.1 *Assessment research demographic information*

Type of course		Description of courses	
Introductory	4	Counselling skills	4
Intermediate	8	Counselling certificate	4
Advanced	25	Diplomas	26
Psychotherapy	3	Masters	3
		Psychotherapy	3
Total	40		
		Total	40
BAC recognized courses	7		
*Orientation		Institutions	
Person-centred	14	University	13
Transactional analysis	1	Higher education	4
Psychodynamic	9	Further education	12
Systemic	7	Private institutions	7
Integrative	12	Voluntary organizations	2
Eclectic	9	Other	2

*Respondents were asked to indicate up to two major theoretical influences on the course they are involved with. Some ticked two boxes and others only one. Hence this table represents the range of theoretical influence.

In order to explore the limits of tolerance of trainers in assessing the competence of their trainees, respondents were asked several questions (see below) about ethical difficulties in relation to assessment and given four brief case studies to comment on. The questions are reproduced here with an analysis of the replies.

In your experience have students passed the course who you and at least one other member of your course team would consider unsuitable to be counsellors?

Of the thirty-four people who responded to this question fifteen (44 per cent) replied that they had passed students who they considered unsuitable to be counsellors. Although space was given for comments few were given in that part of the questionnaire. The most frequent comment from those who responded negatively was that students who were considered unsuitable were screened out of the course in some way before the end. However in response to the next question more detailed comments were made.

Have you ever found yourself in an ethical dilemma as a trainer? If yes, can you describe it?

To this question twenty-five (78 per cent) respondents answered positively and only seven reported no ethical dilemmas (of those two commented that they had not been in the job very long). Of the twenty-five comments, eleven related to difficulties of assessment. Six of the other comments related to difficulties with co-trainers or staff members attending the course. The seven interviewees were asked whether they had ever passed students on their courses against their better judgement. Only one respondent was certain that everyone who graduated from his course (which had very small numbers) was fully competent.

The ethical difficulties that emerged in relation to assessment were centred around students who had been successful in fulfilling the formal criteria for passing a course but whose personality, interpersonal communication or psychological adjustment caused concern. Comments such as: 'I worry about the occasional student on a course who seems to be a bit disturbed. I have a gut feeling that I should ask them to leave but I do not have any concrete evidence to offer'; 'There is a student on the course who is already employed as a counsellor, who in my opinion is neither skilled nor suited to practise. He would not be accepted on to the next stage of the training'; 'Students can be academically bright and able but in our opinion they are not good counsellors'; 'Passing a student who I have not felt OK about despite meeting our criteria.'

Respondents to the questionnaire were also asked:

Can you describe any other uncomfortable student situations that may affect assessment?

A summary of the situations described are listed below:

- Students who are fixed on working with a specific client group, which may include choosing to work with only one sex or one race.
- Students who have personal development needs themselves, who use training to covertly meet or avoid those needs.

- Students who exhibit difficulties with time boundaries relating to attendance, punctuality or giving in assessed work.
- Course members who irritate others or stir up problems for the group.
- Students whose religious or political beliefs spill over into their counselling.
- Students who produce poor tape recorded counselling sessions but good supervision reports.
- Students with study difficulties, particularly those who claim to have dyslexia without producing evidence or who produce fraudulent work.
- Students who are also colleagues in the same institution.
- Students who take on private clients before they are trained sufficiently to do so.
- Students with homosexual or lesbian tendencies.

Examining the list of situations that pose assessment difficulties eight of the ten statements describe aspects of personality, self awareness or personal development and question a trainee's suitability or readiness to undertake the role of counsellor. The problems around assessing a colleague or trusting the integrity of a supervisor may or may not fall into the same realm of self development. The comment about homosexuality is surprising in the context of counselling, although in psychotherapy training there has always been a resistance to accepting homosexual or lesbian trainees.

Four brief descriptions of students who may give trainers cause for concern were fabricated. Three will be recognized from the examples given earlier of students who might be considered a risk at the selection stage. Respondents were given a visual analogue scale on which to estimate how likely each student would be to pass the course and to comment on each one. The descriptions were brief sketches which left much to the imagination but they inspired a wide variety of reactions. The most common response was to confront the person about their behaviour or to recommend personal therapy. It is the author's experience that difficult students are either already in personal therapy or resistant to it. They also tend to be resistant to feedback or confrontation which contributes to the reason that they continue to be difficult.

Case study: Christine

Christine achieves high marks in all her assignments. Her clinical performance is good and she seems to achieve a good relationship with her clients. However on the course she is difficult. She is demanding of special attention from the tutors and tends to rundown other members of the group behind their backs.

How likely is Christine to pass the course?

RESPONDENT SCORES

Mean 50.9   Median 50   Mode 50
Std Dev 33.052   Valid cases 30

Christine inspired a range of responses that illuminate the different methods of assessment that are used by courses. Some courses have definite
strategies for the assessment of personal development and others do not.
When asked in the questionnaire whether they assess personal development
eighteen out of twenty-six (69 per cent) courses reported that they used
formal methods in this respect. Some courses refer to assessment boards
who are empowered to pass, fail or defer on a wide range of criteria: 'the
individual would be referred to the training meeting'. Other courses refer to
stages of training noting that unless Christine made some changes she
would not be allowed on to the next part of the course. Similarly one course
mentions the power to confer UKCP registration at the end of the course,
which would be withheld for unsuitable candidates.

Reference is made in some instances to the type of assignments that are
set or methods of assessment. Self and peer assessment systems were
considered to be more likely to pick up and confront the behaviour that has
been described with the result that Christine would be challenged directly
by others with an option to change or risk failure. Another respondent
claimed that the assignments are set to ensure that students reflect on their
own behaviour and interpersonal style. If their self description differed
significantly from that which tutors observed, students would be unlikely to
pass the assignments.

There were also respondents who suggested that they recognized Christine as the type of student with whom they were familiar and about whom
they had concerns. They suggested that if she passed the assignments she
would pass the course and that perhaps their system of assessment was not
sensitive enough to pick up this kind of problem. The comment was also
made that the longer the problem was ignored the more difficult it would be
to deal with but on the other hand it was important to give students time to
act on feedback and challenges they received. People can change!

Some of the comments raised issues about the assessment of personal
development, particularly the confidentiality of personal development
groups. It would be appropriate for Christine's problem to be challenged by
others in a personal development group but if no assessment of performance
in those groups is made, then her response to challenges cannot be the
subject of assessment. 'We have made the point that the personal development group is not to be assessed and we stick by this.' Many respondents
seemed confident that tutorial help or community processes would deal
with the problem but those with formal assessment procedures that take
account of personal development issues seemed the most confident in their
responses that she could not pass unless she changed. 'The assessment

procedure would confront her behaviour in the first year. She would be expected to resolve this in therapy.'

Case study: Geoff

The second case study raised different issues.

Geoff writes well and relates well to others. His counselling skills are generally good, although he tends to develop a bad stutter when he is under pressure. This has sometimes been a problem in counselling sessions particularly when he is challenged by a client.

How likely is Geoff to pass the course?

RESPONDENT SCORES

Mean 66.70   Median 70   Mode 99
Std Dev 28.34   Valid cases 30

Geoff was the student whose problem received the most sympathy, who was seen as the least problematic and the most likely of the four to pass. Responses to this student were however varied and few addressed the pass or fail issue. Comments fell into several categories, the first being his need to have help to correct his stammer through special tutorials, relaxation training, specialist help or personal therapy. 'As a tutor I would recommend that Geoff enters into personal therapy.' 'Referred for personal remedial work.' The second category included comments about equal opportunities and his right to pass regardless of the stammer. 'Pass or fail would not depend on this factor.' 'On an equal opportunities basis he would pass, but we would recommend he gets help.' The third related to the need to monitor his performance through supervision and to develop skills to manage challenging clients more effectively. 'We would look at this in counselling practice and in consultation with Geoff and his supervisor.' The fourth group commented on his relationship with clients: if that was satisfactory then he should pass. 'He would need to learn congruent responses in relation to his disability.' 'Help would be provided in focusing upon his difficulty with aggression. Not only told to work with it in therapy, but work required with the course.'

Inevitably respondents wanted to know more about the severity of Geoff's problem and were reluctant to comment given so little information. Others seemed optimistic that Geoff could deal with his stammer, perhaps somewhat unrealistic given that for some stammering has been a lifetime problem and is resistant to treatment. However the general response to him was that the problem was not too serious and could be dealt with. The impact of counsellors with disabilities on clients is one that has not received much attention. We might wish that it would make no difference but given the evidence that clients like their counsellor to be keenly attentive, natural and unstudied (Strupp, 1959) or confident and professional (Beutler *et al.*, 1986) someone who stutters particularly in response to emotional confrontation could be unhelpful. In particular given that Geoff's stutter is at its worst in the face of hostility from clients, it is relevant to note Bandura's (1960) observation that the progress of clients in therapy is adversely affected by therapist conflict about accepting client hostility. On the other hand Bliss (1994) writing as a disabled therapist was adamant that her disability had not restricted clients from expressing their anger, fear or distress. At times she perceived it to be of benefit to the client, 'it can be used like Winnicott's spatula – it can be held out for the client to play with if she or he chooses' (p.116). She was turned down in her original application to become a training therapist for a psychotherapy training organization but the decision was reversed on appeal.

Case study: Sophie

The third case study gave respondents cause for concern.

Sophie is a good counsellor in many ways and is extremely conscientious about her work with clients. She is however painfully thin and although she says that she has recovered from anorexia after five years of therapy, she never eats in public and is often away ill.

How likely is it that Sophie will pass the course?

RESPONDENT SCORES

Mean 46.8   Median 56   Mode 50
Std Dev 32.42   Valid cases 30

Of the four case studies presented Sophie was considered to be the least likely to pass the course. There are three dimensions to the problem, her eating disorder, her conscientiousness and the attendance issue, and respondents have tended to focus on one or other of the issues.

Taking the eating disorder first, responses varied between seeing it as a serious problem that had to be resolved: 'We would confront Sophie about her eating problem and ask her to address those issues in therapy, possibly advocating that she take a break from counselling', and criticism of the questionnaire that it should be considered a problem at all, 'I am a good counsellor/trainer and have an eating disorder which I am coping with via counselling. I recognize this as prejudice!' Some respondents found it difficult to engage with the problem given so little information: 'Before pass or fail is decided the issue mentioned would be opened up. I would need to know more about her illness. Difficult to judge her suitability. Are we looking for the perfect person?', and they were irritated by the implication that good counsellors cannot have their own problems: 'I know of many counsellors who suffer from depression, anorexia, etc., and yet they seem to be able to function quite well with their clients.'

Several respondents were concerned about the conscientious description given and interpreted it as a symptom of unresolved difficulties, 'The description of extreme conscientiousness suggests that control issues are unresolved. Something needed to free aggression. Difficult to believe the good counsellor description.' The point was also made that being conscientious does not correlate with effectiveness as a counsellor.

Sophie's attendance provoked the most comments and seemed to be the problem around which respondents were most confident about predicting failure. Attendance is something that can be quantified and hence clear criteria for attendance requirements can be stipulated. Several people mentioned an 80 per cent attendance requirement on their courses, which was supported by follow up interview data. During the interviews two trainers said that they had a 100 per cent attendance requirement and that any sessions missed had to be taken when that session was repeated, possibly the following year, or the work had to be made up by some other means. Some respondents implied that if the student had an attendance problem 'her absences would seriously interfere with her membership of the course and she would probably be asked to defer'.

Again, some respondents recognized students such as Sophie and expressed concern that the system in which they work would allow her to pass because their assessment scheme would not have a means of failing her: 'On an equal opportunities basis she would pass, but I would discuss with her what I would put in references for future jobs.' Many respondents mentioned that Sophie should be referred for personal therapy despite the fact that the case study mentioned that she had already had therapy for five years: 'I think that there would be an understanding that to be vulnerable does not incapacitate a good caring counsellor, but support would be given and discussion about more effective therapy would ensue.' It is an obvious comment for counsellors to make when they have trainees with personal problems but it is questionable whether therapy can always help, particularly within the time span of a two-year counselling training course. Anorexia is notoriously difficult to treat and while some sufferers make a full recovery many continue with their symptoms for years. While no counsellor or therapist is without their unresolved personal issues, some are more visible than others. As in the case of Geoff, the stutterer, despite goodwill towards a student with an eating disorder, the impact of a painfully thin counsellor on a client may impede the development of trust and hence client progress.

Case study: Daniel

The last case study was also quite difficult for respondents to grapple with.

Daniel is a Black probation officer. He has done well on the course but continually challenges staff about the lack of attention paid to Black issues. He has been on placement with an agency offering counselling to Black clients and insists that he is not prepared to see any white clients.

How likely is Daniel to pass the course?

RESPONDENT SCORES

Mean 57.5   Median 56   Mode 50
Std Dev 30.65   Valid cases 30

The case study of Daniel focused on two issues, his challenge to the staff about the lack of focus on Black issues, and his insistence on seeing only Black clients. Some respondents were sympathetic to Daniel but others found the problem worrying, expressed as 'Help! Seriously worrying' or 'Bloody hell!' Comments raised issues of equal opportunities, racism, selection of trainees, placement requirements, confrontation of his views and referral for personal therapy. Equal opportunities, race and cultural considerations are a major source of stress for counselling trainers (McLeod, 1995). While there is often a willingness to address racial issues, in practice trainers, usually white, lack experience and expertise to satisfy students' demands with respect to race and culture, particularly as they wrestle with the task of producing a balanced curriculum.

The respondents who viewed Daniel sympathetically wrote comments such as 'He has a right to choose who he will work with', 'He is as entitled to his racism as the course tutor', 'Who he chooses to see is up to him and his agency.' Some could not engage with the problem from their own experience as their agencies are located in areas where Black clients are rare, or because the course is attached to a counselling agency which has a policy of random allocation of clients, 'He would never have started the course because our trainees are engaged in counselling for our agency and counsellors see whoever walks through the door.'

Several respondents mentioned potential failure. 'Depends on whether this is a personal or political issue. If he was not destructive and incongruent and if he was able to be philosophical, he could well pass. However if it was aggression fired by unresolved personal issues he might fail.' 'He would need sensitive tutoring but if he persisted in oppressive practice he would not pass.' 'While the challenge about racist issues would be welcome, his stipulation about working with one client group would lead to failure to demonstrate core components and hence failure on the course.'

There were several comments about his need for personal therapy, such as, 'There is a shortage of Black counsellors. I would recommend he seek out therapy to sort out his difficulties regarding race.' Others thought that his attitudes would be confronted as part of the group process or through tutorials: 'Before pass or fail is decided, the issue mentioned above would be opened up'. 'Daniel would be able to offer skills but needs challenge *re* possible punitive response to white clients.' Clearly some trainers responding to this questionnaire were uncomfortable with the issues of race raised by this case study. Several mentioned that they had equal opportunities groups, forums or committees to which they would refer this kind of problem. Finally some respondents replied by saying that the issues raised in the Daniel case study would have no effect on assessment: 'Pass or fail would not depend on this factor,' 'Pass or fail depends on assessment of a practice video assignment and supervisor's report.'

The data collected on these case profiles was analysed using Kendall's coefficient of concordance. The scores for each of the four trainees were put into rank order between the most and least likely to pass the course. The total of ranks assigned was:

Geoff: 61   Daniel: 67   Christine: 71   Sophie: 74

Geoff scored as if he was the most likely to pass the course and Sophie the least but the test was not significant. Hence it cannot be concluded that there was any agreement between the trainers about who would or would not pass the course.

The case studies described here were included in a questionnaire to survey the responses of trainers to students who may have personal development needs, the most difficult aspect of trainees to assess. Some assessment has to be made about the trainee's ability to make a relationship with a client without judgement or prejudice and ability to facilitate the client's exploration of a wide range of issues without being handicapped by their own blind spots. The responsibility for being a gatekeeper of the counselling profession is considerable and failing a student at the end of a long and arduous training can be a painful experience for all concerned.

Many interesting issues were raised that have implications for the way in which courses design and organize aspects of assessment. It was clear that most trainers recognized the difficulties presented in the four case studies and would intend to challenge or confront students concerned in some way. Some said that such students would not pass and others that they should not, but that the system they were in may not be able to prevent their success. Assessment systems must be highly complex in order to take account of psychological development of trainees without being persecutory, perceived as biased with judgements based on personal opinions, or infringing rights of confidentiality. Systems that include rigorous self and peer assessment or professional assessment boards to which a wide range of evidence of professional competence is presented may be able to cope with personal development issues of trainees more effectively than systems that rely on pass or fail of prescribed assignments solely.

This research was not designed to make a detailed comparison between competence assessment systems of private counselling training agencies and universities but some anecdotal evidence from the questionnaires and interviews suggest that private agencies, particularly those who also offer counselling, are able to be more flexible in their methods of assessment and are able to take account of personal development issues more systematically. This would make sense because a private agency dealing entirely with counselling and training is likely to be more sensitive to the assessment of counsellor competence than a generic institution with wide-ranging concerns.

Other issues that were raised included selection of students for a training course, information given to applicants both about course requirements and methods of assessment, attendance requirements for successful course completion and agency requirements if counselling is provided by students for the agency. As with assessing competence, trainers are able to devise criteria for selection than can be applied to make decisions about suitability but there are always borderline (not necessarily in the clinical sense) candidates such as those sketched earlier. In such cases the applicant appears to meet the criteria but there are intangible factors such as gut feelings that suggest the person may not be entirely right for the course. Questionnaire respondents suggested that problems on courses can be avoided if students are given comprehensive information about the course and its assessment criteria before they start it. While this is desirable and achievable on paper, students are not always willing or able to take in every aspect of information that could inform their decisions. Attendance requirements can be stated but unless they are always rigidly and unerringly adhered to, there will always be students with exceptional circumstances who challenge the system. There will also be those whose non-attendance is more suspect. Rules about attendance have to be applied universally hence some sympathy for deserving cases is usually built into the system. Less deserving cases sometimes take advantage of a sympathetic approach.

COMPLAINTS AND APPEALS

All institutions offering counselling training should have a system that enables students to appeal against assessment decisions made and a complaints procedure to deal with other matters that cause concern. In counselling agencies an appeals committee would probably consist of people who understand professional issues related to counselling whereas in a generic institution this may not be the case. As a result it may be more difficult in some settings to explain to an appeals board why a particular trainee should be excluded from the course. An uninformed committee may err on the side of giving second chances, when, in the opinion of the counsellor training staff, a student is unsuitable to continue training. However the principle of equal opportunities should always be upheld. The possibility that course tutors (and perhaps peers and others) might be prejudiced against a particular individual will always need to be borne in mind. More information about procedures for fair assessment is given in Chapter 9.

SUMMARY

Counselling training is fraught with difficulties for trainers and students alike. There are times when trainers are faced with difficult decisions about the performance of their trainees as counsellors. A major area of concern is in the realm of personal development. Trainers have varied value systems when it comes to the assessment of counsellor competence. They are helped when they have an assessment scheme that includes formal methods of assessing personal development and clear criteria for making such assessments. However, whichever system is adopted, subjective judgements will always feature in the assessment of trainees and pass or fail decisions will often be made that reflect the trainer's limits of tolerance of what makes a good enough counsellor.

EIGHT

Schemes for assessing competence: NVQs and the rest

INTRODUCTION

Counselling in Britain is an unregulated profession. Anyone can put a sign on their door to offer their services as a counsellor. The public has had little information to help them in the choice of a counsellor, although more has recently been written on this topic (see Cooper and Lewis, 1995). A Directory of Counsellors is produced annually by the British Association of Counselling (BAC, 1996) but no check is made on the competence of those who pay for their entry into this publication. From June 1996 a United Kingdom Register of Counsellors includes the names of counsellors who have met a designated standard of competence either through BAC accreditation or through accreditation offered by the agency or organization for whom they work as counsellors.

Since 1996 two major schemes for assessing the competence of counsellors have existed, BAC Accreditation of Counsellors and National Vocational Qualifications (hereafter referred to as NVQs) both of which will be reviewed in this chapter. Brief reference will also be made to the examination boards that offer qualifications in counselling, namely the Royal Society of Arts (RSA), City and Guilds and Associated Examining Board (AEB). Finally, brief mention will also be made of the United Kingdom Register of Counsellors and the UKCP Register of Psychotherapists.

BAC ACCREDITATION SCHEME

The British Association for Counselling (BAC) developed a scheme for the accreditation of counsellors during the 1980s which has provided a benchmark for professional counselling competence. Details of the scheme as issued by BAC are given below.

BAC ACCREDITATION CRITERIA

These criteria apply only to counsellors working with individuals or couples. They do not apply to group counselling.

There are three routes to Accreditation. The successful applicant will be one who prior to application:

1. i   Has completed a BAC Recognised Counsellor Training Course and has had at least 450 hours of counselling practice supervised in accordance with paragraph 2 below, over a minimum period of three years.

OR

Has undertaken a total of 450 hours of counselling training comprising two elements:

a)   200 hours of skills development
b)   250 hours of theory

and has had at least 450 hours of counselling practice supervised in accordance with paragraph 2 below, over a minimum period of three years.

OR

ii   Is claiming little formal (course based) counselling training, but can provide evidence of seven years' experience in counselling as understood by BAC with a minimum of 150 practice hours per year under formal supervision, and has had at least 450 hours of subsequent counselling practice (supervised in accordance with paragraph 2 overleaf) over three years. (NB: this is a restatement of the 'Ten Year Clause'.)

OR

iii   Can provide evidence of a combination of:
      (a)   some formal counselling training and
      (b)   several years of practice (of 150 hours minimum per year, under formal supervision). This includes a requirement for at least 450 hours of counselling practice supervised in accordance with paragraph 2 below, over three years.

75 hours of completed counsellor training = 1 unit
1 year of supervised practice = 1 unit

Together the total must add up to 10 units.

Applicants claiming two or more training units must show a balance of theory and skills approximately in line with that stated in 1.i above.

In addition to the above, the application is required to meet the following criteria:

2. Has agreed formal arrangements for counselling supervision, as understood by BAC, of a minimum of one and a half hours monthly on the applicant's work, and a commitment to continue this for the period of accreditation.

3. Gives evidence of serious commitment to on-going professional and personal development such as regular participation in further training courses, study, personal therapy, etc.

4. Is a current individual member of BAC and undertakes to remain so for the accreditation period.

5. Has a philosophy of counselling which integrates training, experience, further development and practice. Evidence of at least one core theoretical model should be demonstrated.

6. Demonstrates practice which adheres to the BAC Code of Ethics and Practice for Counsellors and undertakes to continue working within this Code.

Applicants are asked to give evidence of the above in the form of a written application including two case studies. Assessors will be looking for congruence between all parts of the application as well as checking that the above criteria have been and are being met.

(BAC (1994). Reproduced in full with kind permission of BAC.)

The scheme provides a national 'rite of passage' for experienced counsellors. Given the plethora of qualifications and courses that exist in counselling, it gives clients a national standard to refer to when choosing a counsellor. It is an optional scheme that counsellors decide to participate in, and it is one of the routes to inclusion in the United Kingdom Register of Counsellors.

As can be seen from the BAC details reproduced above there are now three routes to accreditation, based on the total number of hours training in theory and skills that a counsellor has had, and a minimum number of hours of practice. Accreditation, if awarded, lasts for five years after which time an application to renew it has to be submitted. It is the method of assessment of competence that is particularly relevant to this chapter.

WHAT IS REQUIRED?

Applicants are required to submit the following: a completed application form which includes full details of all counselling training undertaken; a diary of their counselling work for a recent month, and a summary of counselling practice in the years submitted and details of current counselling practice; a statement about their continuing professional development; a statement of their philosophy of counselling; a case study of their recent work with a client that gives an illustration of counselling philosophy, theoretical orientation, techniques or methods and an account of the counselling process (1,000 words); a second case study which includes an illustration of the content and process of supervision and the integration of supervision and practice (1,000 words); a signed statement from their supervisor; a reference from another person who can comment on their work.

WHO ASSESSES IT?

The assessment of accreditation applications is carried out by teams of four professional counsellors, three assessors and a convenor, on a voluntary basis, who are themselves BAC accredited. The teams are balanced to reflect as wide a range of theoretical orientations as possible.

HOW IS IT ASSESSED?

All applications are carefully scrutinized with close attention being paid to any inconsistencies. Hours of theory and skills training are checked and the diary of counselling work is read to ensure that the counsellor is undertaking counselling as understood by BAC.

The statement of professional development is regarded as an important indicator of the counsellor's awareness of the need to continually update their skills and knowledge. Involvement in at least one professional development activity, such as personal counselling, attendance at seminars, conferences or workshops, reading counselling journals and books, having a role within a professional organization or other activity is expected.

Applicants are required to produce a statement of their own philosophy of counselling, which must demonstrate that they have a clear sense of what they are doing and the theoretical concepts that underpin their approach. This statement is held in mind by the assessor when reading the case studies presented. The philosophical rationale described must be reflected in the case work produced. Inconsistencies perceived may be grounds for failing the application after consultation with the assessment team.

The supervisor's report is seen as a vital part of the accreditation procedure hence details of the supervisor's status, training and experience are collected. The supervisor is the person closest to the counsellor's clinical work, who should be able to comment directly on the quality and professionalism of work with clients. Supervisors are required to discuss their comments with the counsellor. There is an implication in the scheme that supervisors will only recommend counsellors for accreditation when they feel that the counsellor is ready. However that can be difficult for super-visors, who come from a range of different backgrounds, including varied theoretical orientations and professional trainings (Russell and Dexter, 1993) and who may have no way of knowing how the performance of their supervisee compares with others who gain accreditation. The second reference may be from someone associated with the counsellor's work such as an agency manager or colleague.

THE PROCEDURE

Applications for accreditation are accepted by BAC four times each year. Each member of a team reads and assesses each application independently and conveys their decision to the convenor. The convenor is an experienced assessor who has the additional role of collating opinions of the team and taking them to the Individual Accreditation Group meetings where decisions/ratifications are made. This procedure takes approximately three months.

Unsuccessful applicants are given full feedback on their applications identifying all the grounds on which their application has been refused. At this stage they are also given information about appeals, re-submissions and re-applications. In recent years the success rate of applications has increased to about 75 per cent as counsellors have become more aware of the standards required, sometimes as a result of using consultants, experienced as asses-sors for the scheme who can advise and support candidates through the process.

The accreditation scheme has recently been under review (Hooper, 1995). While the scheme itself works well for those who pass through it, the number of accredited counsellors in Britain represents only a small propor-tion of those practising. The United Kingdom Register of Counsellors may encourage many more counsellors to apply for accreditation as that is the only route to registration for individuals not connected to a substantial agency which provides both training and counselling service delivery. BAC was concerned that the current scheme may not be able to cope with a substantial increase in applications and consideration has been given to modifications. At the time of writing it is unknown what changes will be made to the scheme.

CRITIQUE

A debate about the relevance and validity of accreditation has raged through the medium of the BAC *Counselling* journal for many years and elicits passionate polemic (see Howard, Martin, Grant, 1992; Russell and Dexter, 1993; Foskett, 1994). Russell and Dexter argue that despite claims that accreditation gives potential clients a quality control system, awareness of the existence of accredited status amongst the counsellor-seeking public is minimal. Furthermore they argue that the scheme offers poor quality assurance anyway as there are so many loopholes that would allow an unscrupulous and immoral applicant to squeeze through the net. Falsifying documents and commissioning others to help with case studies would not be difficult for someone determined to cheat. Russell (1993) asserts that research into unethical behaviour suggests that accredited counsellors may be just as culpable as others. However the assessment of competence in counsellors is complex and while the BAC accreditation scheme may be less than perfect, it has at least offered a professional standard that counsellors can work towards for their own personal satisfaction of achieving national recognition. Recent developments in the form of NVQs could provide new national standards, which may provide a new benchmark of counselling competence into the next millennium.

NATIONAL VOCATIONAL QUALIFICATIONS

NVQs in Counselling should be available in Britain during 1996. The impact they will have on counselling training and assessment is at the time of writing unknown. The development of NVQs in counselling has involved substantial government expenditure and thousands of hours of effort on the part of counsellors, therapists and consultants in the process. The scheme of awards for people training and working as counsellors or using counselling skills in their work is comprehensive, controversial and as yet untested. The results will be interesting. Here, the intention is to give a brief background to the history and context of the development of NVQs, to give some examples of standards that have been agreed to date, to consider assessment criteria for the attainment of standards and to offer a critique of the strengths and weaknesses of the scheme.

History of the development of NVQs

In October 1992 the Conservative British Government published an intention statement and objectives for NVQ/SVQ (Scottish Vocational Qualifications) (HMSO, 1993):

> In order for the UK to maintain and improve its competitive position in the world and for its work force to have the flexibility to respond to changing economics and markets, the Government is supporting the

NVQ/SVQ initiative. The objective is to confirm and improve the competitive position of the UK work force by:

1) recognising its current skill level, and
2) providing a route for all to improve their skills and the quality of the service they provide.

These aims sound laudable enough but represented yet another move on the part of the government to centralize and control the provision of education and training, this time by the development of national assessment criteria (Hickox, 1995). Ten per cent of the UK work force (2 million people) were identified as having either paid or voluntary work involving advice, guidance or counselling. Hence the Advice, Guidance, Counselling and Psychotherapy Lead Body (AGCPLB) was established to develop NVQs for the identified population. The work of the lead body was divided into five key areas: business enterprise, care and health, counselling and psychotherapy services, support and advisory services, and education, training and work. Psychotherapy, not included in the initial Lead Body briefs; was added when the overlap between counselling and psychotherapy was recognized, and the working group associated with the Counselling and Psychotherapy Services area is of prime interest.

Using specialist consultants, the lead body Standards Development Group (SDG) has prepared draft standards to define areas of competence for advice, guidance and counselling work. Those draft standards have been used as a basis for consultation with the counselling community through workshops, with individual volunteers, via questionnaires to practitioners, in dialogue through counselling journals as well as with other specialist groups set up within the lead body such as the Ethics and Equality group. Consultation led to the revision of draft standards and their subsequent release for field trials, during which 350 practitioners used log books to record how their work marries up with standards in practice.

The first release of standards became available in April 1995. These standards cover the broad area of advice, guidance and counselling. Standards for therapeutic counselling are not available at the time of writing but the general flavour of NVQs can be discerned by what is already known. The standards comprise A Units which are seen as generic to all counselling and guidance work and B Units which are applicable to specialist roles. Work is currently in hand to cluster units together to provide specific qualifications which match broad roles or functions in the workplace. Identified clusters of units will comprise an NVQ. These qualifications will soon be available through awarding bodies approved by the NCVQ (National Council for Vocational Qualifications) or SCOTVEC (the Scottish Vocational Education Council). Assessment of units will take place through approved centres that work in conjunction with the awarding bodies. The awarding bodies for advice and guidance NVQs are currently City and

Guilds, the Local Government Management Board (LGMB) in conjunction with the Institute of Careers Guidance, SCOTVEC and the Open University.

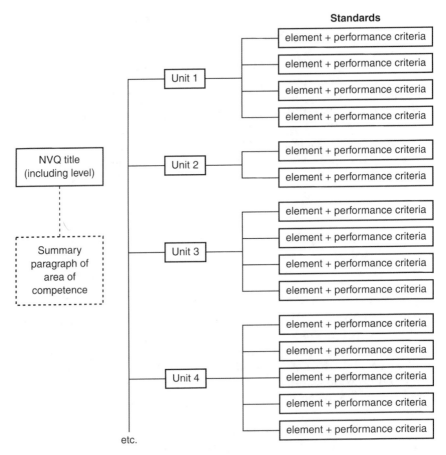

Figure 8.1 *The structure of National Vocational Qualifications*
Source: Wolf (1995). Used with permission.

Much of what follows has been gleaned from Wolf (1995) whose excellent book on competence-based assessment is recommended for the reader who wants to understand more about the development of NVQs than it is possible to recount in part of one chapter. She has defined competence-based assessment as 'a form of assessment that is derived from the specification of a set of outcomes; that so clearly states both the outcomes – general and specific – that assessors, students and interested third parties can all make reasonably objective judgements with respect to student achievement or non-achievement of these outcomes; and that certifies student progress on the basis of demonstrated achievement of these outcomes. Assessments are not tied to time served in formal educational settings' (p.1). Encapsulated in this definition are three components of competence-based assessment in the NVQ scheme:

- the emphasis on outcomes
- the belief that these can be specified into minute detail which are transparent and can clearly be assessed by third parties
- the separation of assessment from any institution or course of learning

Wolf describes how competence-based assessment has been derived from a broader notion of criterion-referenced assessment, an American concept which has influenced the development of the National Curriculum in schools since the late 1980s. The primary difference between the two systems is that criterion-referenced assessment would usually include assessment through examinations or other paper and pen exercises, whereas competence-based assessment is focused on performance or outcome in tasks as they are performed in the workplace.

Competence-based assessment found favour with the Conservative Government at a time of mass youth unemployment in the 1970s and early 1980s when emergency programmes including work experience were created to occupy the young. A form of assessment was perceived to be needed for what people could do, rather than for what they knew, a challenge to the existing system of assessment of the time which was largely knowledge-based, e.g. General Certificate of Secondary Education (GCSE). Jessup (1991), a major proponent of competency-based testing, has written scathingly about what he describes as a 'provider led system', education that is driven by a syllabus that ignores the needs of the learner and suggests that the only reliable measure of attainment is what someone is observed to be able to do. He suggests that a competence-based assessment gives the learner direct access to information about what is required and gives them autonomy to decide at what point they are ready to offer themselves for assessment.

Figure 8.2 summarizes the changes that have taken place in the nature and structure of vocational qualifications. It is important to note that 'the process of NVQ accreditation does not involve any formal discussion of curriculum (except in so far as it is implicit in the standards) or approval of learning programmes. The assumption is that the use of standards will ensure the latter's quality. It is part of NCVQ policy that awards should not be tied to course attendance or "time serving"' (Wolf, p.16). Given what has been discussed earlier in Chapter 6 concerning personal development and the benefit to students of having an experience of being with a group of students over a period of time, who gain confidence to challenge problems or blind spots, an assessment scheme which detaches itself totally from a learning experience is worrying in the realm of counselling training. The

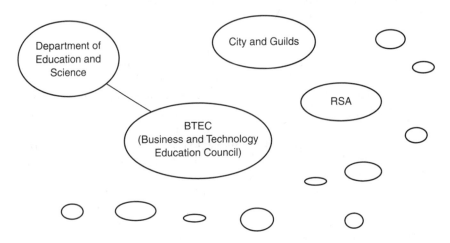

Before reform: myriad self-regulating awarding bodies

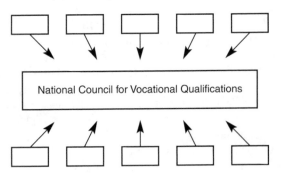

After reform: lead bodies (representing industries) submit standards to NCVQ for approval

National Council for Vocational Qualifications

Awarding bodies submit qualifications based on standards to NCVQ for approval

Figure 8.2 *Vocational qualifications system in England and Wales before and after reform*
Source: Wolf (1995). Used with permission.

system will need to be very sensitive indeed to take account of the depth of personal development that is required to sustain competent performance in all circumstances.

The award of an NVQ represents competence in a defined area of work at a specific level. There are five levels; levels 1–4 have been prescribed and 5 is meant to take account of competence beyond level 4. The levels do not relate to years of study but to the nature of the associated work role. Descriptions attached to levels are given here (NCVQ (1995) *NVQ Criteria and Guidance* (p.11)):

LEVEL 1

Competence which involves the application of knowledge in the performance of a range of varied work activities, most of which may be routine or predictable.

LEVEL 2

Competence which involves the application of knowledge in a significant range of varied work activities, performed in a variety of contexts. Some of the activities are complex or non-routine and there is some individual responsibility or autonomy. Collaboration with others, perhaps through membership of a work group or team, may often be a requirement.

LEVEL 3

Competence which involves the application of knowledge in a broad range of varied work activities, most of which are complex and non-routine. There is considerable responsibility and autonomy and control or guidance of others is often required.

LEVEL 4

Competence which involves the application of knowledge in a broad range of complex, technical or professional work activities performed in a wide variety of contexts and with a substantial degree of personal responsibility and autonomy. Responsibility for the work of others and allocation of resources is often but not necessarily present.

LEVEL 5

Competence which involves the application of a significant range of fundamental principles across a wide and often unpredictable variety of contexts. Very substantial personal autonomy and often significant responsibility for the work of others and for the allocation of substantial resources feature strongly, as do personal accountability for analysis and diagnosis, design, planning, execution and evaluation.

At the time of writing the levels at which NVQs in counselling are to be offered are not known. Descriptions of levels 4 and 5 imply that the person satisfying the conditions for an award at that level would occupy a role, or at least be competent to occupy a role at management level. Hence it is likely that management units will form part of any NVQ that is offered in counselling at these levels. (See Figure 8.1.)

This may not be appropriate for counsellors who have a depth of clinical skill and competence but who have no interest in managing a service. At the same time professional clinical counselling practitioners may not be satisfied with awards at level 3 or below. The relevance of this definition of levels of competence to counselling and psychotherapy is questionable.

To put the discussion of NVQs for counselling in context it might be useful to refer to an example.

Figure 8.3 shows one of two elements that make up Unit A.3. A combination of units would contribute to an NVQ qualification. As can be seen from the performance criteria in Element A.3.2 each one is outcome-based, described using an active verb and an object.

It must be noted that the performance criteria are absolute; the atmosphere *is* created. The notion that the counsellor has an awareness of difficulties and endeavours to create a safe atmosphere is absent from the description. A developmental approach is eschewed in favour of the requirement for demonstration of total success. There are many circumstances in which the most experienced counsellors would have difficulty in creating such an atmosphere with some clients. The atmosphere is not totally within the counsellor's control.

The range statements for this element are in some senses contradictory; they suggest that there are circumstances when support will be necessary. It may be difficult to create a safe atmosphere when the client threatens the counsellor, who would then be correct to seek help and support, but the client may not then have 'an opportunity to explore their issues and concerns at their own pace'.

The knowledge specification for this element is considerable and constitutes a syllabus of what needs to be learned to be deemed competent. However, the evidence requirement example given is quite a simple one; observation (direct or indirect) of enabling clients to identify issues and concerns. No direct assessment of the extent to which the knowledge base has been assimilated is suggested. This should be implicit in the behaviour observed. When the range statements are taken into account, the trainee counsellor would have to be observed in many different circumstances for the assessor to be certain that they would behave appropriately and competently in all the circumstances indicated.

Wolf summarizes the requirements for competence-based assessment in the NVQ system as follows (p.21):

1. *One to one correspondence with outcome based standards.* This must be comprehensive: evidence must be collected to show that a candidate has met every single performance criterion. Failure to do this, it is argued, removes an essential characteristic of the system – the fact that we know exactly what someone who has been assessed can do (or at least has once been able to do).

2. *Individualized assessment.* Candidates should be able to present themselves for assessment on relevant criteria and elements as and when they are ready to do so, and the necessary assessment and

ADVICE, GUIDANCE, COUNSELLING & PSYCHOTHERAPY LEAD BODY
FIRST RELEASE STANDARDS

Unit A.3 Develop Interaction with Clients

Element A.3.2 Enable clients to identify issues and concerns

PERFORMANCE CRITERIA

a) An atmosphere is created in which clients feel safe enough to express their issues and concerns
b) Clients are provided with an opportunity to explore their issues and concerns at their own pace
c) Situations requiring immediate action are identified and appropriate action promptly taken
d) Clients' requirements beyond own competence and organisation's boundaries are identified and appropriate action agreed and taken
e) Support is sought from a suitable person where there are difficulties in working with clients
f) The interaction is brought to an end in a positive manner when clients' immediate concerns have been met

RANGE

1. Support sought due to: immediate risk situation; limits of own competence; effect of own values, beliefs, life experience and reactions to clients.
2. Taking into account effect of own values, beliefs and life experience in relation to: awareness of own cultural, social and gender identity, sexuality, age and experience; identification of own prejudices, blocks and stereotyping.
3. Situations requiring immediate action: risk to clients, practitioners, others; clients' immediate physical, emotional and practical needs.

KNOWLEDGE SPECIFICATION

- Organisation's policy and procedures for service delivery
- Limits of the organisation
- How to communicate effectively with individual clients
- Likely constraints to communication and how to minimise them
- Characteristics of a safe atmosphere, including psychological safety and the impact of the environment
- Ways of creating a safe environment
- Own limitations and appropriate sources of support
- Impact of own attitudes, values and behaviour on work with clients
- Equal opportunities legislation and good practice
- Organisation's equal opportunity policy and code of practice
- Equality of opportunity and non-discriminatory practice with regard to developing interaction with clients
- Differences between practitioner and clients, their implications and ways of dealing with them
- Issues of risk and personal safety, and ways of dealing with them
- Sources of and procedures for referral
- Issues of and organisation's policy on confidentiality

EVIDENCE REQUIREMENTS

Observation (direct or indirect) of enabling clients to identify issues and concerns

Evidence Routes to follow

Figure 8.3 *Unit A.3: Element A.3.2*

recording systems set up to allow such 'assessment on demand'. This implies that sophisticated systems for APL (Accreditation of Prior Learning) must be made available.

3. *Competent/not yet competent judgements only.* Grading is rejected, there is a pass/fail for each element and any notion of how individuals perform in comparison to others is irrelevant.

4. *Assessment should be in the work place whenever possible.* Alternatively, conditions as close as possible to those under which counselling would normally be practised must be created.

5. *No specified time for completion of assessment.*

6. *No specified course of learning/study.*

These requirements have many attractive and welcome aspects. The opportunity to gain qualifications based on experience that are open to all, is valuable. Little is yet known about the cost of NVQ assessment but if fees are kept low, it may be of great advantage to some who are unable to meet the ever-growing expense of counsellor training. There are also some difficulties. The syllabus of study may be derived from the outcome competencies. This could lead to courses being geared towards NVQ assessment, without a substantial foundation in a core theoretical model on which skills can be developed. Dryden (1992) debated whether counsellors should be educated or trained, whether the focus of learning should be the acquisition of knowledge or skills, and concluded that it was essential to include both. While knowledge requirements are specified in the NVQ Units, interpretation of how comprehensive that knowledge needs to be is left with the individual. It is possible that a candidate may be able to demonstrate skills without understanding what they are doing. 'What distinguishes higher education from other levels of education, it is argued, is that the knowledge towards which students aspire, . . . and the skills they acquire, are necessarily provisional, half formed, indeterminate – and so problematical. As a result, students have to become critical thinkers. Competence, in contrast, implies that the relevant knowledge can be sufficiently complete to be operationalized into identifiable skills, which is difficult to reconcile with permanent problematization' (Scott, 1995, p.162).

Given that there are no time limits on choosing to be assessed, or limits on the number of times a candidate can present themselves, some may suffer. Determination to succeed in the face of adversity is commendable but a candidate could present themselves for assessment repeatedly at considerable personal cost, both financial and in terms of self esteem, if they are unable to achieve the required standards.

A substantial problem that is raised for counselling in the NVQ scheme is the process of assessment. All assessors must have formal training in NVQ assessment techniques, indeed must achieve an NVQ in assessment. The scheme encourages assessment in the workplace, through competence demonstrated on the job. For counsellors, this process is not straightforward. Interviews between counsellor and client are confidential and not open to public scrutiny. Counselling agencies are usually small and whereas a large company may have its own trained NVQ assessor, small organizations are unlikely to have one. Even if an assessor exists within an organization, Wolf has illuminated the potential conflicts that can arise when one colleague assesses another in the same team. Teams need to work together, compensating for each other's strengths and weaknesses, which might be complicated by the awareness of being assessed, particularly as the competencies do not have shades of success but are described only as pass or fail.

Time taken for the process of assessment poses a challenge to assessors whether they are based in a workplace or at an accredited centre.

Element B.7.1. as shown in Figure 8.4 is one of four elements of Unit B.7 entitled 'Develop the counselling relationship'.

Under ideal circumstances, over a period of several years in a busy counselling practice, it might be possible, through regular individual clinical supervision, to be sure that a candidate for assessment had met all the requirements. The assessment of element B.7.1 would take a considerable amount of assessor's time. If the portfolio of evidence required was presented at an assessment centre it would similarly take time for the assessor to go through the work with the candidate as well as possibly providing an opportunity for an observed role play session or two. The assessor would have to be a skilled and experienced counsellor as well as having the NVQ in assessment. In some subjects Wolf reports anecdotal evidence that more time is given to assessment than to the development of learning in that subject. She also notes that some evidence suggests that comprehensive assessment is impossible and that the process has to be fudged to produce results.

The performance criteria for units, as they are written and the pass/fail (described in NVQ terms as competent/not competent) only outcome of assessment implies that to be successful the person being assessed has to achieve mastery. They have to achieve 100 per cent to pass, and to be successful in all the performance criteria. This is unrealistic. An element of judgement on the part of the assessor about how good is good enough is inevitable. 'Any form of assessment involves activity and judgement on the assessor's part – whether it be examining a PhD, listening to a music examination candidate or observing a care assistant . . . . All the research evidence that we have on assessor's behaviour emphasizes the very active role that their own concepts and interpretations play' (Wolf, 1995, p.67) She describes assessors as having 'an internalised, holistic set of concepts about what an assessment ought to show, and about how, and how far, they can take account of the context of the performance, make allowances, refer to other evidence about the candidate in deciding what they "really meant" ' (p.65). Anyone who has ever listened to the tape recording of a trainee

ADVICE, GUIDANCE, COUNSELLING & PSYCHOTHERAPY LEAD BODY
FIRST RELEASE STANDARDS

Unit B.7 Develop the Counselling Relationship

Element B.7.1 Enable clients to identify issues and concerns

PERFORMANCE CRITERIA

a) Clients are enabled to express their concerns freely

b) Presenting issues are explored with clients in order to establish their nature and depth and attention is paid to the possibility of underlying issues

c) Situations requiring immediate action are identified and appropriate action promptly taken

d) Clients are enabled to identify own primary concerns in relation to the presenting issues

e) Clients are enabled to prioritise concerns to be worked on

f) Material outside clients' awareness is brought into their awareness and their handling of that material facilitated

g) Markers signifying strong emotional reactions are identified and responded to appropriately

RANGE

1. Nature of concerns: presenting issues; precipitating factors; related but different concerns/issues; unrelated but relevant concerns and issues; relationship between client's inner and outer world; relationship between client's past, present and future.

2. Enabling clients to express concerns: giving full and undivided attention; demonstrating receptiveness; finding a shared language; reflecting back and mirroring; checking understanding of what has been said; affirming significance of what is being said; paraphrasing and summarising; respecting the chosen position of the other person and matching own position to that of client.

3. Situations requiring immediate action: risk to clients, practitioner, third parties; client's immediate physical, emotional and practical needs.

KNOWLEDGE SPECIFICATION

- Ethical codes of practice and principles underpinning practice
- Equal Opportunities legislation and good practice
- Equality of opportunity and non-discriminatory practice with regard to the counselling setting
- Organisation's equal opportunities policy and code of practice
- Models of counselling and relationship to individual theoretical perspective
- Models of person and identity development within differing social and cultural contexts
- Patterns of human integration and separation
- Procedures to secure and maintain confidentiality including note-taking, record-keeping and identity protection
- Special conditions which compromise confidentiality and consequences for conduct of sessions incuding protection of third party and over-riding legal duty on counsellors, as well as common law precedent, judges' conventions, and custom and practice, including disclosure to third parties
- Own role within the organisation
- Limits of own competence and responsibilities
- Signs and symptoms of mental illness

EVIDENCE REQUIREMENTS

Feedback from formal supervision with witness testimony from supervisor

Client case notes in relation to development of counselling relationship with evaluative commentary on ways in which clients are enabled to identify concerns

Evaluative commentary on own practice showing way in which counselling and communication skills are used to enable clients to identify concerns

Personal logs of counselling with particular reference to developing counselling relationship

---

Evidence Routes to follow

Figure 8.4 *Unit B.7: Element B.7.1*

counsellor in action will know exactly what she means. The assessor takes account of the candidate's anxiety at having a tape recorder present and of being assessed. They will hear all the mistakes and balance them alongside the good things that they are witness to. At the end of the tape they will think about the client, their material, the counsellor, the climate and atmosphere of the session as well as skills demonstrated. Sometimes it is easy to make a clear pass or fail decision, but the middle ground is the problematic decision-making arena. In the NVQ scheme the absence of proof of competence in one of the performance criteria implies failure, a tough decision for the assessor to make.

The NVQ scheme claims fairness to all candidates because assessment is made against specific criteria which can be interpreted by all who read them. However specific these definitions might be when assessing counselling ability, as no doubt with other subjects, there is room for subjectivity in the assessment process. This might be further complicated by the variety of assessors involved, who may come from different counselling training backgrounds and have varied levels of experience. To ensure the best possible quality control of assessment decision-making, assessors will have to meet and cross-reference some of their assessments, adding another time commitment to their schedule, although one essential to good practice.

The NCVQ (National Council for Vocational Qualifications) is determined that quality assurance of NVQs will be maintained. To quote NVQ criteria and guidance (NCVQ, 1995, p.40):

6.1 NCVQ has an overriding responsibility for ensuring that awarding bodies have adequate arrangements and resources for quality assurance and that systems approved at the time of accreditation operate effectively and maintain the required performance throughout the period of accreditation. It will therefore require awarding bodies to:

6.1.1 ensure the availability of sufficient competent assessors and verifiers:

6.1.2 monitor or verify that assessment is operated in accordance with their requirements and consistently maintained at all assessment locations:

6.1.3 select, train, certificate and review the performance of external verifiers:

Internal verifiers are responsible for advising assessors and for maintaining the quality of assessment in a centre. National standards are assured by the use of external verifiers appointed by the awarding body. Assessors, internal and external verifiers work together through an approved centre to a Common Accord which establishes standard terms for their roles and functions in the assessment and verification system. Time alone will tell how well these systems will work for counselling assessment.

Response to the development of NVQs in counselling from practitioners has been mixed. Large numbers of professional counsellors have given their time to the development of standards and will be influenced by their experience of that process, both positively and negatively. Foskett in *Counselling* (1994) in describing his response to the development of counselling standards said 'Counselling can only be standardised if we want to produce statues, and people won't stand still' (p.138). In the same article he says that 'he favours a system of accreditation which is not fixed or final, embraces politics, beliefs and values as well as behaviour, trusts a degree of overlap, incoherence and chaos, and is suspicious of a surfeit of consistencies.' Anecdotal evidence and that gleaned from research interviews conducted by the author during 1995 suggest that counselling trainers have a mixed response to NVQ. Higher education-based courses may be indifferent to these new qualifications because they are secure in the credibility given by the strength and reputation of their organizations, but smaller private institutions may be keen to offer routes to qualifications that have national standing, providing that the reputation of NVQs turns out to be positive. Association with NVQ will provide them with free publicity as the amount of money spent on the scheme to date seems to be a bottomless pit.

In summary it is fair to say that the assessment of competence in counselling is a complex process and no ideal scheme has yet been developed. At the very least an enormous amount of time, money, effort and expertise has been invested in the development of NVQ standards; it will be interesting to see whether they become the backbone of counselling training, accreditation and certification during the next decade.

WHAT ELSE IS THERE?

There are examining bodies in Britain that have been awarding qualifications in counselling for many years although none claim to be offering a qualification that can be deemed to imply competence to practice independently as a counsellor. The RSA Examining Board has offered certificates in counselling skills in the development of learning (RSA, 1984) for many years. City and Guilds have offered certificates in counselling skills and are now one of the awarding bodies for NVQs in advice and guidance. The AEB (Associated Examining Board) have also offered qualifications in counselling, which have been taken up by private organizations that do not have the national standing to award their own certificates and diplomas. Of course, universities have always awarded their own qualifications and counselling is now included amongst them, but little can be generalized from the standards achieved on such courses as they vary considerably (Wheeler, 1994). There are also consortia of organizations that meet to set standards in counselling such as CENTRA, based in Manchester.

Finally mention must be made of systems operated by the BPS (British Psychological Society) and the UKCP (United Kingdom Council for Psychotherapy), particularly as counselling and psychotherapy are being brought together through the development of NVQs and the boundaries may become more blurred rather than more distinct in the future. BPS offers a qualification in Counselling Psychology, leading to chartered counselling psychologist status. This qualification is offered to counsellors who have a psychology degree and who undertake a prescribed course in counselling psychology offered at various universities throughout Britain. In contrast to most organizations described earlier the UKCP does not offer a qualification but operates a register of psychotherapists. The route to inclusion on the register is through organizations that are accepted as members. These organizations provide psychotherapy training which is vetted prior to acceptance into membership of UKCP. Students who satisfactorily complete training at a member organization qualify for inclusion on the UKCP register, which is deemed to provide a kite mark of competence.

CONCLUSION

It is difficult to conclude a chapter such as this at this time. There are so many changes in the development of nationally recognizable qualifications that imply counselling competence. The BAC Accreditation Scheme is under review, NVQs are just beginning to emerge and the United Kingdom Register of Counsellors has just opened. The BPS Counselling Psychology courses are relatively new and the examination boards are fighting for a market share in the counselling awards arena. In the updating of this book in five years' time, this chapter will have to be rewritten entirely as the various schemes develop or decline. There is no doubt that regulation of the counselling profession through competence standards is here to stay.

NINE

Quality assurance: external accountability and evalution

The assessment of competence of counsellors or the organization of it is primarily the responsibility of the staff team involved with a counsellor training course. Many aspects of assessment have been considered including what to assess, how to assess and who should assess students. The course staff will be involved with assessment to a lesser or greater degree depending on the core theoretical model used for the training, but the role that should be common to all professional training courses is that of the external examiner, who monitors the assessment decisions made. Courses should also engage in their own monitoring and evaluation process. They should seek to provide the best possible learning experience for their students, which results in their competence to practise as counsellors. Just as in counselling itself, there is no room for complacency and course evaluation is just as important as the evaluation of counsellor competence through assessment.

EXTERNAL EXAMINER

The external examiner to a course should really be 'external', a person who is competent themselves as a counsellor, has an understanding of the theoretical orientation taught but who has no other involvement with the course. The staff, through documentation, should be able to clearly articulate their expectations of students, the standards they are expected to reach, the assessment tasks involved and criteria for successful accomplishment, which can then be made available to both students and the external examiner. Given that everyone then knows what is expected it should be possible for the external examiner to make judgements about whether the staff or students and their peers are being fair in the assessment decisions they make.

A counselling course community can be intense. Close relationships develop and because of the nature of the subjects studied and the practical work undertaken, all participants, staff and students, get to know each other very well. While efforts to ensure impartiality when marking students' work are made, it is not impossible for personal perceptions of an individual, favouritism or prejudice to creep into the process. It is the external examiner who ensures fair treatment for all, because such a person should not have prior knowledge of any students or personal involvement with any member of staff. They should be able to judge the work of students with impartiality.

An external examiner will usually be nominated by a staff team based on knowledge of the person from meetings in a professional context such as conferences or committees or by recommendation from others. The external examiner should under no circumstances be a personal friend or relative of any member of the course staff. The appointment will usually be made by the organization employing the staff and the external examiner is accountable to the organization. External examiners are usually appointed for a fixed period of not more than five years. More than one external examiner may be appointed to a course if it has a large number of students.

The precise nature of the role of an external examiner will vary between institutions but what follows is a list of possible functions described by Dryden, Horton and Mearns (1995, p.138).

1. While external examiners will normally not be expected to become involved in the actual marking of students' work, they may be asked to approve the procedures and content of the assessment scheme.

2. External examiners receive a previously agreed number and representative sample of each of the written assessment items. The sample would include any borderline pass/fail and pass/distinction or equivalent borderline categories. The external examiner would moderate the standard and consistency of the internal marking. Most external examiners would expect to receive a copy of the guidelines and criteria given to students, together with a copy of the staff feedback given to each student in the sample and a complete mark list for the particular cohort of students.

3. The external examiner may need to visit the course to observe any form of practical work assessment.

4. Some counselling courses require an oral examination as part of the formal assessment procedure, but even where it is not a formal requirement, some institutions recognise that the external examiner has the right to conduct a viva voce examination if he or

she so wishes. However, it is normal for this to be used only to confirm or improve a candidate's marks.

5.   The external examiner should be involved in discussion relating to any student who may be required to withdraw from the course because of unsatisfactory progress or failure to achieve the required standard of work or who displays conduct that is considered to be unethical or unprofessional.

6.   The external examiner is usually consulted about any proposed changes to the assessment scheme.

COURSE CONSULTANT

A course may also choose to have a consultant, who is not involved directly with assessment but more with evaluation and development of the course. A course consultant would have an arrangement with the staff team to have regular meetings, financed by the course budget. The purpose of the meetings would be to offer support, advice and feedback to the team on any aspect of the course that is raised. They might discuss the effective functioning of the staff team, issues that are raised through the evaluation of the course by staff, students or external examiner, future developments or difficulties encountered with particular students or the umbrella institution.

PEER PARTNERSHIP

The BAC Course Recognition Scheme (BAC, 1996) has evolved its own system of evaluation and peer review through partnerships. Each recognized course is given another recognized course with whom to form a partnership. Information about all aspects of the courses are exchanged and regular meetings are held between the core staff members. The purpose of these meetings is to become familiar with the partner course and its personnel. Items for discussion might include course evaluation, assessment schemes, selection, equal opportunities, institutional issues, staff changes, appeals and complaints as well as the trials and tribulations of running a recognized course.

This partnership scheme has proved to be a valuable resource in a process of peer review. It provides an opportunity for staff to reflect on issues that arise or on course development with external professionals with a vested interest in providing feedback and support. The reciprocal nature of the process encourages openness and honesty. At the end of the five years of recognition, courses apply for re-recognition, at which time the annual reports produced by the partner course form a major part of the submission. Failure to meet and participate in the peer review process would be a reason for not granting re-recognition. The peer partnership scheme provides an effective means of evaluating the training provided.

EVALUATION OF TRAINING

It is the aim of professional counsellor training courses to facilitate the development of their students to become competent counsellors and to provide the best possible programme of study through which staff and students can meet their objectives. The level of achievement attained by students at the end of a counselling course may be a reflection of the quality of training or could be attributed to their natural talent as counsellors. Poor outcome could be a product of poor selection of candidates in the first instance. Counsellor training courses are expensive in terms of time and money. No expense should be spared to evaluate the effectiveness of all aspects of a training programme, to ensure that time and money are spent for maximum benefit. In a way assessment of competence of counselling trainees is a measure of the effectiveness of a course and hence an evaluation of it, but it only provides a picture of the course from one angle and comprehensive evaluation requires a multi-faceted approach.

Quality assurance is a key phrase of the 1990s (Dryden *et al.*, 1995) and all echelons of higher education are subject to internal and external audit. Departments are required to carry out their own annual internal audit and external audit takes place periodically organized through the Higher Education Funding Council (England) (HEFCE). The audit process seeks to monitor all aspects of educational provision including administrative arrangements and procedures, selection criteria and process, curriculum planning, assessment procedures, equal opportunities, quality of teaching and tutoring, facilities for students and course completion and success rates. In addition the audit process concerns itself with evaluation procedures, monitoring the requirement that all courses have such procedures in place. A hastily constructed questionnaire at the end of a two-year course would not be enough.

Evaluation of training courses can serve many purposes. Regular routine evaluation may elicit information that can be used to make changes that have an immediate impact on current students to improve their training experience. Retrospective or summative evaluation can only be used for the benefit of future students. Evaluation also has an important contribution to make to the body of research on counsellor training, highlighting innovations that have a positive impact on the development of competence as well as casting doubt on practices that are shown to be ineffective. Alternatively its fruits can be discarded into filing cabinets to gather dust providing benefits for only dustmites and filing cabinet manufacturers.

Evaluation instruments or procedures need to be carefully designed and regularly used, but managed sensitively. Just as students may be anxious about assessment, 'staff can feel vulnerable to potential criticism and threatened by the prospect of negative judgements being made about them and their work' (Dryden *et al.*, 1995, p.145). Evaluation needs to be a collaborative venture between staff and students that is a vehicle for communication, encouraging an open dialogue that can be constructively used to inform future practice, rather than a secretive venture that allows unspoken hostility and dissatisfaction a destructive voice. At the same time evaluation procedures must be kept in perspective, acceptable to staff and course members equally, not becoming an overwhelming burden for staff or an irritant for students (Firth *et al.*, 1993).

INTERNAL AUDIT

Dryden, Horton and Mearns (1995) have given an account of what might be investigated as part of an internal audit of a counselling course. They suggest that the following data should be collected:

- number of applications received, applicants interviewed, places offered and places accepted
- number of students in each cohort or year group, drop outs and reasons for leaving
- number of students passing the course
- information on employment changes of students as a result of taking the course
- student feedback and evaluation including summary of comments
- external examiner's report or evaluation
- staff response to critical feedback from students or external examiner
- changes or solutions to problems during the year
- proposed developments or improvements for future courses
- staff professional and academic development activities
- extra-ordinary achievements of the course or students
- organizational problems beyond the responsibility of the staff team

From the data collected an audit report can be written that serves to demonstrate the standards achieved by the course and to make it accountable to the organization sponsoring the course as well as its students. There may be instances when the audit report can be used pro-actively in order to negotiate for resources or changes from the host organization.

WHAT ASPECTS OF THE COURSE COULD BE EVALUATED?

There are numerous aspects of a course that could be the focus of evaluation including teaching methods, effectiveness of particular staff, skills packages, theoretical content, supervision, personal development in general, groupwork or therapy in particular, individual workshops, cross-cultural counselling, assessment process and outcome to name but a few. Many academic papers have been written about various aspects of evaluation a few of which are mentioned briefly here.

SKILLS

The counselling model which has prompted the most evaluative research has been the micro-skills counselling model developed by Ivey (1971). The model offers training in discrete skills which are taught systematically. Trainees' counselling interventions can be observed and recorded before and after training and results have been consistently positive in showing that students are more able to demonstrate these skills after training than pre-training measures indicate (Ivey and Authier, 1978; Hargie, 1986).

Rushton and Davis (1992) have reported the evaluation they undertook of a sixty-hour course to train community health professionals in the basic skills of counselling families of children with disabilities. They used the didactic-experiential programme of Truax and Carkhuff (1967) to teach the course. They had the advantage of a control group of students, who were on a waiting list to participate in the training, and after comparing the skills demonstrated with families of the trained and untrained groups, concluded that the course was cost effective in enhancing the counselling skills of those who attended.

Gallagher (1993) used the Problem Solving Inventory (PSI) developed by Heppner and Petersen (1992) to measure aspects of the personal problem solving process. Students undertook a 25-week programme of problem solving/problem management training based on Human Resource Development, Interpersonal Process Recall and Microcounselling (Baker *et al.*, 1990). The inventory was administered before and after training and results concluded that students' problem solving effectiveness had improved.

In practice few counselling courses offer a recognized package of skills that have been the subject of other studies. However, given the suggestion made earlier that it is good practice for courses to have target competencies or skills that students know they are expected to achieve, it need not be too difficult to organize exercises or questionnaires that measure these competencies or skills, pre- and post-training. Even crude measures or instruments can be valuable to show students the progress they have made and to demonstrate to the institution the effectiveness of training, even if they do not lend themselves to scrutiny from a wider audience, lacking validity and reliability.

THEORETICAL CONTENT

One of the traditional ways in which the assimilation of course content is evaluated is through the use of examinations. Firth *et al.* (1993) sought to evaluate a course in psychodynamic counselling using performance indicators (measures of change in objective knowledge by timed examinations) and preference indicators (attitudes relating to assessment, course structure and content, etc). The evaluation format was a 'before and after' design. Students took an examination at the beginning of the course and again at the end. The written examination included definitions, multiple choice questions and short answers. Significant differences in scores were recorded before and after the training.

THE STUDENT EXPERIENCE OF THE COURSE

When it comes to the evaluation of student experience there is no substitute for asking the students to report regularly, either in written or verbal format, using numerical ratings or not. For the purpose of analysis a questionnaire that itemizes all aspects of the course and requires a rating for each aspect is a convenient system to adopt. A sample evaluation form for one term of a course is given in Appendix C. It is useful to include space for written comments and particularly to ask for suggestions for improvement. Some suggestions will always be impractical. A course of indefinite length might satisfy everyone, except that some would complain about its length. It is important to be able to deduce from feedback, essential topics that have been omitted or given insufficient attention. Stevenson *et al.* (1984) noted that students on clinical psychology training programmes report that practical clinical training is perceived to be the most valuable part of their training and is frequently considered to be the least adequate. Such observations through evaluation have led to changes in training priorities. Students offer valuable information about their experience of training, some of which can be used in producing agendas for staff development or for confronting institutions with the specific needs of counselling courses.

TEACHING METHODS

There is always a personal dimension when the evaluation of teaching methods is considered. Such evaluation can be perceived as threatening to the teachers or trainers involved, because of anxiety about job security and personal criticism. It is not always easy to distinguish between teaching method and the competence of the teacher. Some teachers/trainers/ lecturers will inspire and excite students using a traditional teaching method such as a lecture and be acclaimed by all, whereas another will be criticized for lacking in initiative or creativity for delivering information in that format. Student feedback can be hurtful and it behoves the training team to structure evaluation exercises in such a way that the information elicited can be used as a focus for team and course development activity.

Trainers need to be aware of their strengths and weaknesses, in order that their strengths can be fully utilized and that their weaknesses can be the focus of a programme of personal and professional development. Students will feel encouraged if they perceive that their comments are taken seriously and acted upon, even if improvements are not immediate.

The BAC *Code of Ethics and Practice for Trainers* (1995a, A2.2 and 2.3) states:

> A 2.2 Trainers must monitor their training work and be able and willing to account to trainees and colleagues for what they do and why.
>
> A 2.3 Trainers must regularly monitor and evaluate the limits of their competence as trainers by means of regular supervision or consultancy.

Dryden *et al.* (1995) have modified a self evaluation check list from Rowntree (1981, p.281), which they suggest that staff use regularly to monitor their own performance as trainers. Their list is as follows: Was the accommodation suitable (e.g. seating arrangement)? Was the session carefully planned? Did the plan prove appropriate? Were the objectives clear to the students? Was the content well structured? Was the time available adequate to cover all aspects of the topic? Were the methods and media appropriate? Were the methods and media used successfully? Was the 'social climate' conducive to learning? Did students participate appropriately? Am I satisfied with what was learned? Do I think the students were satisfied with what they gained from the session? How do I know? What would I do differently another time?

Dryden *et al.* (1995) suggest that staff evaluate their teaching sessions regularly, perhaps once every two months. They may discuss their teaching with a consultant or mentor, other members of the staff team or even engage in peer evaluation through which they regularly sit in on a colleague's teaching session and use their observations as a basis for discussion. Despite good intentions there are opportunities for complacency and collusion. Involving a course consultant in the evaluation of teaching and in consideration of students' feedback can be helpful. They can then facilitate open discussion with the staff in a supportive way and even help with the constructive resolution of tensions that might arise for the teaching team.

SUPERVISION

Clinical supervisors may be members of the staff team or may be individually contracted by students and have little or no contact with the course. Hence, there are numerous questions that can be asked about supervision. Are the arrangements for supervision adequate, given the nature of the training and client work and the amount of client work required? Are appropriate supervisors chosen? Are they adequately trained and qualified for the job they are doing? Is the information given to supervisors about the course adequate? Do supervisors have any feedback to give to the course about students selected, course curriculum, methods of assessment, placement requirements, their role in assessment, level of competence achieved by students or their role in relationship to the course? How satisfied are students with their supervisors? What impact do they feel that supervision has on their client work? How important is supervision for students as part of their training? A sample evaluation form used by students to evaluate their supervisor and supervision is given in Appendix D.

PERSONAL DEVELOPMENT

While all aspects of counsellor training courses can promote self development there are usually components that are specifically described as self development activities. This includes personal therapy, groupwork and the use of learning journals or diaries (see Chapter 6). While such activities are generally reported to be beneficial, formal evaluation can reveal interesting information that is worthy of consideration.

Personal therapy is regarded as an essential aspect of psychotherapy training and is encouraged, if not required, for counselling trainees. The rationale is that therapists need to have explored their own difficulties in order to be open to the concerns of their clients. They need subjective experience of being a client to inform their awareness of the therapeutic process from the client's perspective. However, in 1988 Macaskill reviewed the empirical literature on personal therapy in the training of psychotherapists and found no evidence to support the assumption that personal therapy is likely to contribute to effectiveness as a therapist. Surprisingly this trend was confirmed in a study by Wheeler (1991) who found a negative correlation between the number of years that counsellors had had personal therapy and their therapeutic alliance scores with clients with eating disorders. She went on to discuss the relative merits of personal therapy for counselling trainees, concluding that therapy can have a distracting affect on trainees as they become immersed in their own pathology, a distraction from their work with clients.

Many courses include a personal development group experience in the curriculum, facilitated by a regular member of the course team or an external group leader, depending on the core theoretical model of therapy adopted. Some research studies have attempted to evaluate the effectiveness of such groups including O'Leary *et al.* (1994), Small and Manthei (1988) and Izzard and Wheeler (1994). O'Leary developed the work of Small and

Manthei in designing a study to investigate the outcome of a personal growth group. They used the Semantic Differential Scale (Osgood *et al.*, 1957) and the Rosenberg Self Esteem Scale (Rosenberg, 1965) as pre- and post-measures for a group of students on a Diploma in Guidance and Counselling. They found that levels of self esteem showed a significant increase after participation in the personal growth training group, as measured by the Rosenberg scale and gathered qualitative data that offered more information about the trainees' experience. Five significant components of growth were identified, namely, self awareness, congruence, spirituality, attention to positive and negative feelings and the perception of growth as a dynamic process.

Izzard and Wheeler (1994) have written about the methodological difficulties that emerge when trying to evaluate the effectiveness of a personal development experience and highlight the range of influence that such a group can have on individuals. None the less counsellor trainers should not be deterred from designing an evaluation for such an experience. Groups are resource intensive, requiring low staff/student ratios and high time commitment. Their value and effectiveness as a component of the development of counselling competence warrants attention.

A MULTICULTURAL FRAMEWORK

Reference was made earlier in this work to the development of multicultural counselling skills and counsellor trainers are aware of the need to provide a curriculum that takes account of the multicultural context in which counsellors work. Trying to evaluate to what extent a course is effective in raising awareness of cultural and racial issues and preparing students to be competent counsellors in a multicultural society is not an easy task. Bimrose and Bayne (1995) have reported their evaluation of the effectiveness of the multicultural module included in the Diploma in Counselling they taught. They surveyed ex-students of the course by asking them to keep a diary over a period of weeks in which they recorded incidents during which the multicultural framework offered by the course was helpful or unhelpful.

WHO SHOULD EVALUATE?

It is inevitable that the major burden of evaluation will be carried by the training course staff. Unless an institution-generated evaluation scheme is imposed on them by their umbrella organization or an external body, the initiative for designing and structuring evaluation will rest with staff. Help with the design of an evaluation scheme can be sought from course consultants, external examiners, students, past and present, partner course (see partnership scheme for BAC course recognition), supervisors, group facilitators, administrators, course staff and consumers of counselling services, the clients.

It could be argued that a comprehensive evaluation of a counsellor training course would be incomplete without some evaluation from clients of the effectiveness of the counsellors the course has trained. Such a suggestion immediately invites discussion of the difficulties of evaluating the effectiveness of counselling which is beyond the scope of this book (see Bergin and Garfield, 1994). Pre- and post-counselling measures of client problems or symptoms such as the General Health Questionnaire (GHQ) (Goldberg, 1981) or the Symptom Check List (SCL 90) (Derogatis, 1983) can provide some information about counselling effectiveness (bearing in mind that clients might have improved even if they had not had counselling). Unsophisticated data on client satisfaction with counselling or their perception of the counsellor's competence can make a valuable contribution to a course evaluation portfolio.

HOW SHOULD IT BE EVALUATED?

Various methods of evaluation have already been discussed under a different heading. Methods chosen will depend on the nature of the activity to be evaluated and rigour that may be required. Evaluation studies that have been scientifically designed have much to contribute to the currently sparse body of knowledge about the effectiveness of counsellor training. Even informal feedback from students can contribute to the refinement or development of good training. Methods of evaluation may vary depending on whether it is part of a formative or summative process, whether it is for internal or external perusal, formally required or informally sought.

Structured review, check lists, observation and the use of questionnaires are suggested by Dryden *et al.* (1995) as methods of evaluation data collection. A meeting of students to consider and feedback on their experience of the course might constitute a structured review, during which check lists or questionnaires could be used, as well as taking notes of verbal feedback. Check lists can be produced that invite agreement or disagreement with various statements about the course, such as 'The course prospectus provided an accurate description of what the course entailed' or 'The course has provided clear information about the competencies I am expected to achieve.' Students can be asked to rate their experience of aspects of the course on a five-point scale. Questionnaires can be designed to elicit answers to a wide range of questions from each respondent. It might include tick boxes, open-ended questions, multiple choice questions and space for commentary. What is most important is that the information gathered is such that it can be analysed and used. Time spent designing the perfect evaluation questionnaire is wasted if time and resources are not allocated to collating and discussing the data. Observation may be part of a staff peer review scheme as described above in the section on teaching methods.

MANAGING APPEALS AND COMPLAINTS

Course evaluation, external examiners, course consultants and peer review with a partner course provide important elements of quality control for the delivery of training and assessment of students. However, although these systems are in place there will still be a need for courses to have both an appeals procedure and a complaints procedure. Appeals relate to assessed work and complaints relate to any other aspect of course procedure, including selection, organization and conduct of staff. Appeals and complaints procedures should be available to all students.

Appeals can normally be made in accordance with published regulations about decisions that are made about a student's progress between one part of a course and another, about failure of the course or a particular item of assessment. 'An appeal may usually be made on the grounds that the assessment procedures failed to accord with the Assessment Scheme regulations or that the Assessment Board failed to take proper account of any mitigating circumstances. In most institutions in educational settings, appeals cannot be entertained on matters of academic judgement' (BAC, 1995c, p.3). Academic judgement is usually deemed to be reasonable through the external examination procedure. If pass or fail of a piece of work is in doubt, such work would be given to the external examiner for another opinion. In some settings an appeals board would be unlikely to have the specific expertise required to re-mark an assignment but can investigate procedures. Counselling training courses that are organized by private agencies which are not part of a wider body will need to pay particular attention to appeals criteria, to ensure that objective decisions can be made on procedural grounds, rather than by re-assessing work produced.

A complaints procedure is required by all organizations offering counsellor training, in order that complaints can be addressed internally in the first instance. The complaints procedure should be designed to offer an independent hearing of complaints about ethical or professional issues from students or other members of the public in contact with the course. It would be used when informal meetings have failed to resolve the difficulties or the conflict.

The need for an 'independent' hearing will determine the nature of the complaints procedure. If a course is part of a large organization, such as a college or university, there will be people within that organization who are not involved with the course who can hear complaints. If a course is part of a small private agency providing counsellor training, they will need a procedure that includes the use of an ombudsman or external complaints mediator. A sample complaints procedure is given in Appendix E.

SUMMARY AND CONCLUSION

Despite ending this book with details of complaints procedures, it is hoped that some of the information presented will contribute to the development of fair and just systems of competence assessment that do not lead to complaints. The assessment of competence in counsellors is a complex, demanding and stressful process. It is possible that the rigorous development of National Vocational Qualifications will make it more straightforward but it may not. Designing and organizing a counsellor training course is an arduous and exacting task. If some of the ideas about assessment described here are useful then these words will not have been wasted.

APPENDIX A

The University of Birmingham School of Continuing Studies MEd in Counselling

ASSESSMENT IN SUPERVISION

At the end of the academic year, an assessment will be made of the student's clinical aptitudes, using the forms attached. For each item, the student will receive a mark and verbal feedback comments.

The evaluation will consist of marks that add up to an overall grade – pass/fail/distinction. Students must achieve a pass grade in *each* of the three sections – clinical insight, clinical practice and counsellor self-development.

A fail in any section would mean an overall fail, and the student may be required to repeat a year of supervised practice and take the assessment again.

Halfway through the year there will be a trial run of the assessment process, where the student will receive formative feedback on their progress.

The following notes help to explain the categories used for evaluation purposes:

A. Clinical Insight

1. *Formulation of client's issues*
   This will reflect the student's ability to grasp and understand the client's core issues, and make links with relevant theoretical concepts.
2. *Identification of objectives and therapeutic strategies*
   This will be a measure of the student's ability to plan therapeutically. That is to identify essential aspects of the client's material that have to be taken up and addressed.

3. *Tracking of counselling process*
   This will reflect the student's awareness of moment to moment counselling process as well as the overall progress of the client, the recognition of defence mechanisms and the way the client uses them, and changes that the client makes in relation to the counsellor or the outside world.

4. *Sensitivity to client/counsellor relationship issues*
   This will reflect the counsellor's understanding of transference and countertransference. It may include consideration of fusion, differentiation and empathy issues.

5. *Understanding of how the generic characteristics of counselling and therapy may clash with the cultural values of their client*
   This will reflect the counsellor's ability to grasp the aspects of psychodynamic theory that cause difficulty when dealing with clients who are not White European, or those of a gay/lesbian orientation, and to think creatively around that tension.

B. Clinical Practice

(As far as possible this section should be used to assess actual counselling practice, as heard on audio tapes, in the supervision sessions.)

1. *Self presentation*
   The student's ability to present themselves to the client as a competent professional, conveying confidence, self assurance, non-defensiveness and an ability to cope with whatever is presented by the client.

2. *Therapeutic alliance*
   The student's ability to engage in a therapeutic alliance with their clients that will sustain their work and relationship despite the development of a negative transference.

3. *Structure and pace*
   The student's ability to time their interventions in a way that the client can make the best use of them, and to pace the sessions with sensitivity.

4. *Maintenance of therapeutic boundaries*
   The student's ability to keep their boundaries in the sessions and deal with boundary issues thrown up by the client. This may include issues of self disclosure, and the counsellor's handling of communication with the client outside the sessions.

5. *Appropriate use of technique*
   This will include active listening, avoidance of closed questions, reflection, focusing and appropriate interpretation.

6. *Clarity of communication*

This measures the counsellor's ability to respond clearly and concisely to client material. Responses should not contain jargon, or be mystifying, but should be accessible to the client.

7. *Confrontation*

This reflects the counsellor's ability to tackle issues that are threatening to them or the client, to challenge behaviour and confront contradictions, while still maintaining a good therapeutic alliance.

8. *Awareness of and ability to work with racial/cultural differences*

This reflects the student's ability to recognize when an intervention is inappropriate and to actively seek ways of relating more effectively. It also measures the student's knowledge of communication style differences.

9. *Ability to perceive, formulate and use the countertransference*

This measures the student's willingness to explore their feelings in relation to the client, also their capacity to formulate and put into practice, interventions which reflect the client's impact on the student's inner world.

10. *Ability to perceive, formulate and use the transference*

This reflects the student's ability to read the client's unconscious or conscious communication which relates to how the client experiences being with the student. It also covers the student's ability to formulate interventions which communicate an understanding of the client's experience in this way.

C. Counsellor Self Development

1. *General motivation in the supervision*

This reflects the student's interest in the supervision process, preparation for sessions, commitment, and openness to ideas.

2. *Openness to self exploration*

This measures the student's interest and motivation to reflect on their own issues and development that are stimulated by client material. It does not mean that the supervision session is used for personal therapy, but does indicate that the student uses their self awareness to learn more about the counselling process.

3. *Receptivity to feedback*

This measures the student's ability to absorb and use feedback from the client, the supervisor or their supervision partner and will be observed through changes that may be made after such feedback.

4. *Willingness to examine cultural heritage, etc.*

This reflects the student's openness to explore their own experience of being part of a racial/cultural grouping and how they have both experienced and been part of oppression, racism, discrimination and stereotyping.

Final evaluation feedback process
Supervisors will complete the evaluation form before their last meeting with the students, and will give them to them at that meeting, explaining in more detail their feedback. Students are invited to complete the form themselves making an evaluation of their own performance. Students will have an opportunity to add comments to the supervisor's form. The forms will then be sent to the External Examiner, and the marks will be reported to the Examination Board.

Feedback on supervision
Students are invited to give feedback to their supervisors on their style of supervision and helpfulness to the student. Again a trial run through occurs midway through the year.

APPENDIX B

The University of Birmingham School of Continuing Studies MEd in Counselling

SUPERVISION EVALUATION OF STUDENT PERFORMANCE FORM

Name of Student: Date:
Name of Supervisor:

MARKS

A. Clinical Insight

1. Formulation of client's issues   1 2 3 4 5 6 7 8 9 10

   ....
   ....

2. Identification of objectives and therapeutic   1 2 3 4 5 6 7 8 9 10
   strategies

   ....
   ....

3. Tracking of counselling process   1 2 3 4 5 6 7 8 9 10

   ....
   ....

4. Sensitivity to client/counsellor relationship   1 2 3 4 5 6 7 8 9 10
   issues

   ....
   ....

5. Understanding of how the generic   1 2 3 4 5 6 7 8 9 10
   characteristics of counselling and therapy
   may clash with the cultural values of
   their client

   ....
   ....

B. Clinical Practice

1. Self presentation   1 2 3 4 5 6 7 8 9 10

....

....

2. Therapeutic Alliance   1 2 3 4 5 6 7 8 9 10

....

....

3. Structure and pace   1 2 3 4 5 6 7 8 9 10

....

....

4. Maintenance of therapeutic boundaries   1 2 3 4 5 6 7 8 9 10

....

....

5. Appropriate use of technique   1 2 3 4 5 6 7 8 9 10

....

....

6. Clarity of communication   1 2 3 4 5 6 7 8 9 10

....

....

7. Confrontation   1 2 3 4 5 6 7 8 9 10

....

....

8. Awareness of and ability to work with   1 2 3 4 5 6 7 8 9 10
   racial/cultural differences

....

....

9. Ability to perceive, formulate and use the   1 2 3 4 5 6 7 8 9 10
   countertransference

....

....

10. Ability to perceive, formulate and use the 1 2 3 4 5 6 7 8 9 10
    transference

....

....

C. Counsellor Self Development

1. General motivation in the supervision 1 2 3 4 5 6 7 8 9 10

....
....

2. Openness to self exploration 1 2 3 4 5 6 7 8 9 10

....
....

3. Receptivity to feedback 1 2 3 4 5 6 7 8 9 10

....
....

4. Willingness to examine their own cultural 1 2 3 4 5 6 7 8 9 10
   heritage and explore differences between themselves
   and other cultural/racial/religious/sexual groups

....
....

Scores

Section A............................... (pass mark = 25)
Section B............................... (pass mark = 50)
Section C............................... (pass mark = 20)

Overall Grade: PASS/FAIL/DISTINCTION

COMMENTS:

Scores

150–190	A	69–85	D
109–149	B	BELOW 68	F
86–108	C		

The University of Birmingham School of Continuing Studies MEd Counselling Year I – 1995/96 Evaluation Form

MODULE 1.2 – INTRODUCTION TO PSYCHODYNAMIC THEORY AND PRACTICE – SPRING 1996

Please rate each seminar according to how much you feel that it informed your thinking about the topic, and on the presentation of the seminar.

No value   0........1........2........3........4   Very valuable

Rate presentation similarly:

Poorly presented   0........1........2........3........4   Well presented

Please add any comments you have about the session.

	VALUE	**PRESENTATION**
1. Object Relations Theory and Practice		....
2. Kleinian Theory and Practice	....	....
3. Jungian Theory and Practice I	....	....
4. Jungian Theory and Practice II	....	....
5. Countertransference	....	....
6. Transference	....	....
7. Residential Weekend	....	....

8. The Therapeutic Alliance. Student led ....

....

9. Defence Mechanisms ....

....

10. Regression ....

....

11. Projective Identification ....

....

12. The Therapeutic Frame and Review ....

....

Please comment on the following:

Research Methods Sessions ....

....

....

Counselling Skills Sessions ....

....

....

Personal Tutorials ....

....

....

Please comment on any other aspects of the course ....

....

....

Is the course so far meeting your expectations? ....
If not why not? ....

....

....

Your name (optional) ....

Please return this form on the last day of term

Supervisor Evaluation and Feedback Form

Supervisor: ....

Student: .... Date: ....

		Not at all									Definitely
1.	*Has your supervisor helped you with*										
a)	formulation of client difficulties?	1 2 3 4 5 6 7 8 9 10									
b)	insight into client difficulties?	1 2 3 4 5 6 7 8 9 10									
c)	boundary issues in counselling?	1 2 3 4 5 6 7 8 9 10									
d)	therapeutic strategies?	1 2 3 4 5 6 7 8 9 10									
2.	*Has your supervisor been supportive*										
a)	when you have had difficulties with a client?	1 2 3 4 5 6 7 8 9 10									
b)	when you have had personal difficulties that have had an impact on understanding the client?	1 2 3 4 5 6 7 8 9 10									
3.	*Has supervision helped you*										
a)	to refine or develop your skills?	1 2 3 4 5 6 7 8 9 10									
b)	to gain understanding of psychodynamic counselling?	1 2 3 4 5 6 7 8 9 10									
c)	with issues of race/gender/culture in your counselling work?	1 2 3 4 5 6 7 8 9 10									
4.	*Do you see your supervisor's approach to counselling as being congruent with the rest of the course?*	1 2 3 4 5 6 7 8 9 10									
5.	*How would you rate supervisor's clinical judgement and skill?*	1 2 3 4 5 6 7 8 9 10									
6.	*Please use this space to make any further comments*										

Each supervisee should give one copy of this to their supervisor and a second copy to the course organizer.

APPENDIX E
Model Complaints Procedure

All counsellor training courses should have an appeals procedure and a complaints procedure. Both should be given to students at the beginning of the course and be available to them at all times.

The Appeals Procedure will relate to issues concerning performance in course assessment, passing, failing and grades, exclusion from the course, etc. A sample appeals procedure is not included here as many institutions have their own complex arrangements that cover a wide variety of courses.

The Complaints Procedure will exist to deal with issues relating to the conduct of the course staff and to the organization of the course. It will be a forum for dealing with breaches in Codes of Ethics for trainers, supervisors or counsellors as described by BAC. This is a model or sample complaints procedure which courses might use as a basis for developing their own procedure based on local requirements and conditions.

X TOWN COUNSELLING DIPLOMA COURSE COMPLAINTS PROCEDURE

1. This procedure exists for the use of past or present students on the course, visiting lecturers or others closely associated with the course.
2. Regular time must be set aside for student groups to meet without staff present to discuss course issues. Whenever possible complaints about the course and/or staff should be formally discussed at these meetings. Individuals also have the right to make complaints.
3. Whenever possible complaints about the course or the course staff should be taken up with the principal course organizer or other members of the course staff team. It is sometimes helpful to put the complaint in writing.
4. The course may have a staff/student consultative committee which meets at regular intervals (probably termly) at which complaints and suggestions can be discussed.

5. It may be helpful to appoint an ombudsman for the course to receive complaints, particularly in a small organization. This person should have knowledge of and perhaps peripheral involvement with the course, but should not be a member of the core staff team. The name, address and telephone number of this person must be publicized. The ombudsman should be a counsellor and familiar with the BAC Codes of Ethics. One suggestion is that the ombudsman could be nominated from the recognized course partner or agreed partner.

6. If a complaint is not satisfactorily dealt with by the course staff team within a period of six weeks, then the complaint should be made in writing to the ombudsman.

7. On receipt of the complaint the ombudsman should inform the principal course organizer that a complaint has been received and the nature of the complaint.

8. Within 21 days the course organizer will send their response to the complaint to the ombudsman, and give details of action taken.

9. There may then follow a limited period of written communication, not exceeding 28 days, between the ombudsman and the parties concerned in order to clarify aspects of the documentation. Meetings may also take place if the ombudsman deems it to be appropriate.

10. On the basis of the information received the ombudsman will make a recommendation about the complaint and inform all parties of this decision.

11. The recommendation made by the ombudsman may include advising the complainants to send their formal complaint to the BAC Complaints Panel. The ombudsman may choose to communicate with the BAC Complaints Panel with the information gathered. The ombudsman may decide to inform the principal of the umbrella organization for the course of the complaint with recommendations for action.

12. The course will normally respect the recommendation of the ombudsman, although it may also be bound by wider institutional appeals procedures, particularly related to academic judgement.

13. Complaints may at any time be sent to the BAC Complaints Panel, bypassing the ombudsman.

Name, address and telephone number of the ombudsman:

(Sue Wheeler, May 1995)

References

Advice, Guidance, Counselling and Psychotherapy Lead Body Secretariat (AGCLB) (1995) *First Release of Standards*. AGCLB, 40a High Street, Welwyn, Herts, AL6 9ER.

Alberts, G. and Edelstein, B. (1990) 'Therapist training: a critical review of skill training', *Clinical Psychology Review*, **10**, 5, 497–511.

Allen, J. (1990) 'Counselling psychologists and counsellors: new challenges and opportunities', *British Journal of Guidance and Counselling*, **18**, 3, 321–5.

Allen, T. W. (1967) 'Effectiveness of counselor trainees as a function of psychological openness', *Journal of Counseling Psychology*, **14**, 1, 35–40.

Anchor, K. (1977) 'Personality integration and successful outcome in individual psychotherapy', *Journal of Clinical Psychology*, **33**, 245–6.

D'Andrea, M., Daniels, J. and Heck, R. (1991) 'Evaluating the impact of multicultural counseling training', *Journal of Counseling and Development*, **70**, 143–50.

Atkins, M. J., Beattie, J. and Dockrell, W. B. (1993) *Assessment Issues in Higher Education*. London, Department of Employment.

Atkinson, D. and Shein, S. (1986) 'Similarity in counseling', *The Counseling Psychologist*, **14**, 319–54.

Aveline, M. (1992) 'The use of audio and videotape recordings of therapy session in the supervision and practice of dynamic psychotherapy', *British Journal of Psychotherapy*, **8**, 4, 347–57.

BAC (1985) *Counselling: Definition of Terms in Use with Expansion and Rationale*. Rugby, British Association for Counselling.

BAC (1990) *Code of Ethics and Practice for Counsellors*. Rugby, British Association for Counselling.

BAC (1994) *Counselling Accreditation. Accreditation Criteria.* Rugby, British Association for Counselling.

BAC (1995a) *Code of Ethics and Practice for Trainers in Counselling and Counselling Skills.* Rugby, British Association for Counselling.

BAC (1995b) *Training in Counselling and Psychotherapy: A Directory* (11th edition). Rugby, British Association for Counselling.

BAC (1995c) *Information Sheet, Counsellor Training Courses: External Roles and Procedures.* Rugby, British Association for Counselling.

BAC (1996) *The Recognition of Counsellor Training Courses.* Rugby, British Association for Counselling.

Baker, S. B., Daniels, T. G. and Greeley, A. T. (1990) 'Systematic training of graduate level counselors: narrative and meta analytic review of three major programs', *The Counseling Psychologist*, 18, 282–312.

Bandura, A. (1984) 'Recycling misconceptions of perceived self efficacy', *Cognitive Therapy and Research*, 8, 231–55.

Bandura, A., Lipsher, D. H. and Miller, P. E. (1960) 'Psychotherapists approach-avoidance reaction to patients' expressions of hostility', *Journal of Consulting Psychology*, 24, 1–8.

Barak, A. and Lacrosse, M. B. (1975) 'Multi-dimensional perceptions of counselor behavior: replication and extension', *Journal of Counseling Psychology*, 24, 288–92.

Barnett, R. (1994) *The Limits of Competence.* Buckingham, SRHE and Open University Press.

Barrett-Lennard, G. T. (1962) 'Dimensions of therapists' response of casual factors in therapeutic change', *Psychological Monographs*, 76, (whole no. 43).

Barrett-Lennard, G. T. (1986) 'The relationship inventory now: issues and advances in theory, methodology use', in Greenberg, L. and Pinsoff, W. (eds) *The Psychotherapeutic Process: a research handbook.* New York, Guildford Press.

Baxter, J. C., Brock, B., Hill, P. C. and Rozelle, R. M. (1981) 'Letters of recommendation: a question of value', *Journal of Applied Psychology*, 66, 296–301.

Beck, A. T. *et al.* (1979) *Cognitive Therapy of Repression: A Treatment Manual.* New York, Guildford Press.

Bergin, A. E. and Garfield, S. L. (1994) *Handbook of Psychotherapy and Behaviour Change* (4th edition). New York, Wiley.

Bergin, A. E. and Jensen, J. P. (1989) 'Religiosity of psychotherapists: a national survey', *Psychotherapy*, **27**, 3–7.

Bernard, J. M. and Goodyear, R. K. (1992) *Fundamentals of Clinical Supervision*. Boston, Allyn and Bacon.

Berven, N. and Scofield, M. (1980) 'Evaluation of professional competence through standardised simulations: a review', *Rehabilitation Counseling Bulletin*, **179**, 178–202.

Beutler, L. E., Crago, M. and Arizmendi, T. G. (1986) 'Therapist variable in psychotherapy process and outcome' in Garfield, S. L. and Bergin, A. E. *Handbook of Psychotherapy and Behaviour Change* (3rd edition). New York, Wiley.

Bimrose, J. and Bayne, R. (1995) 'A multicultural framework in counsellor training: a preliminary evaluation', *British Journal of Guidance and Counselling*, **23**, 2, 259–64.

Birtle, J. and Buckingham, C. (1995) 'A cognitive model of assessment' in Mace, C. *The Art and Science of Assessment in Psychotherapy*. London, Routledge.

Bliss, S. (1994) 'Perfection or preconception – some thoughts on reactions to disability in the therapist', *British Journal of Psychotherapy*, **11**, 1, 115–19.

Bond, T. (1993) *Standards and Ethics for Counselling in Action*. London, Sage.

Bowman, J. T. and Roberts, G. T. (1979) 'Effects of tape recording and supervisory evaluation on counselor trainee anxiety levels', *Counselor Education and Supervision*, **19**, 1, 20–6.

Boyd, E. M. and Fales, A. W. (1983) 'Reflective learning: key to learning from experience', *Journal of Humanistic Psychology*, **23**, 2, 99–117.

Bradely, J. and Post, P. (1991) 'Impaired students: do we eliminate them from counselor education programs?', *Counselor Education and Supervision*, **31**, 100–8.

Brady, J. L., Healy, F. C., Norcross, J. C. and Guy, J. D. (1995) 'Stress in counsellors: an integrative research review', Chapter 1 in Dryden, W. *The Stresses of Counselling in Action*. London, Sage.

Bray, D. (1982) 'The assessment centre and the study of lives', *American Psychologist*, **37**, 180–9.

Brown, S. and Knight, P. (1994) *Assessing Learners in Higher Education*. London, Kogan Page.

Buckley, P., Karasu, T. B. and Charles, E. (1981) 'Psychotherapists' view of their personal therapy', *Psychotherapy: Therapy, Research and Practice*, **18**, 299–305.

Carkhuff, R. R. (1969) *Helping and Human Relations: Volume 1, Selection and Training*. New York, Holt, Rinehard and Winston.

Casement, P. (1985) *On Learning From the Patient*. London, Tavistock.

Chevron, E. and Rounsaville, B. (1983) 'Evaluating the clinical skills of psychotherapists', *Archives of General Psychiatry*, **40**, 1129–32.

Clark, M. M. (1986) 'Personal therapy: a review of empirical research', *Professional Psychology*, **17**, 541–3.

Clarkson, P. (1995) 'Counselling psychology in Britain – the next decade', *Counselling Psychology Quarterly*, **8**, 3, 197–204.

Coltart, N. (1988) 'The assessment of psychological mindedness in the diagnostic interview', *British Journal of Psychiatry*, **153**, 818–20.

Coltart, N. (1993) *How to Survive as a Psychotherapist*. London, Sheldon Press.

Combs, A. W. (1986) 'What makes a good helper? A person centred approach', *Person Centred Review*, **1**, 51–61.

Combs, A. W. and Soper, D. W. (1963) 'The perceptual organisation of effective counselors', *Journal of Counseling Psychology*, **10**, 222–7.

Connor, M. (1994) *Training the Counsellor, An Integrative Model*. London, Routledge.

Cooper, J. and Lewis, J. (1995) *Who Can I Turn To? The User's Guide to Therapy and Counselling*. London, Hodder and Stoughton.

Corrigan, J. D. and Schmidt, L. D. (1983) 'Developing and validations of revisions in the Counselor Rating Form', *Journal of Counseling Psychology*, **30**, 64–75.

Crandall, R. and Allen, R. (1982) 'The organisational context of helping relationships' in Wills, T. A. (ed) *Basic Processes in Helping Relationships*. New York, Academic Press.

Crits-Christoph, P. and Mintz, J. (1991) 'Implications of therapist effects for the design and analysis of comparative studies of psychotherapies', *Journal of Consulting and Clinical Psychology*, **56**, 460–95.

Crouch, A. (1992) 'The competent counsellor', *Self and Society*, **20**, 22–5.

Davis, J. (1989) 'Issues in the evaluation of counsellors by supervisors', *Counselling*, 31–7.

Derogatis, L. R. (1983) *SCL – 90: Administration, Scoring and Procedures Manual for the Clinical, Psychometric Research* (revised version). Baltimore, Clinical Psychometric Research.

Dijkstra, C. (1986) 'Over de voorselectie van Rogeriaanse therapeuten', *Tijdschrift voor Psychotherapie*, **12**, 4, 209–25.

Donnan, H. H., Harlan, G. E. and Thompson, S. A. (1969) 'Counselor personality and level of functioning as perceived by counsellees', *Journal of Counseling Psychology*, **16**, 482–5.

Dryden, W. (1993) *Counsellor Training or Counsellor Education. Reflections on Counselling*. London, Whurr.

Dryden, W., Charles Edwards, D. and Woolfe, R. (1989) *Handbook of Counselling in Britain*. London, Routledge.

Dryden, W., Horton, I. and Mearns, D. (1995) *Issues in Professional Counsellor Training*. London, Cassell.

Efstation, J., Patton, M. and Kardash, C. (1990) 'Measuring the working alliance in counselor supervision, *Journal of Counseling Psychology*, **37**, 3, 322–9.

Eliot, R. (1985) 'Helpful and non helpful events in brief counseling interviews: an empirical taxomony', *Journal of Counseling Psychology*, **32**, 307–22.

Engels, D. W. and Dameron, J. D. (1990) 'The Professional Counselor. Competencies, Performance Guidelines and Assessment (2nd edition). Alexandria, USA, American Association for Counseling and Development.

Firth, M. T., Huxley, P. T., Joseph, P. J., Margison, O. and Margison, F. (1993) 'Quantifying creative encounters: the bumpy road to evaluating psychodynamic training', *Journal of Social Work Practice*, **7**, 1, 63–72.

Ford, J. D. (1979) 'Research on training counselors and clinicians', *Review of Educational Research*, **49**, 1, 87–130.

Foskett, J. (1994) 'Whither are we led and by whom? A reaction to Ménage à trois', *Counselling*, **5**, 2, 137–9.

Frank, J. D. (1973) *Persuasion and Healing: A Comparative Study of Psychotherapy*. Baltimore, John Hopkins Press.

Gallagher, M. S. (1993) 'Evaluation of an integrative approach to training paraprofessionals in counselling using the problem solving inventory', *Counselling Psychology Quarterly*, **6**, 1, 27–38.

Gallagher, M. S. and Hargie, O. D. W. (1989) 'An investigation into the validity of role play as a procedure for counsellor skill assessment', *British Journal of Guidance and Counselling*, **17**, 2, 155–65.

Garfield, S. L. and Bergin, A. E. (1971) 'Personal therapy, outcome and some therapist variables', *Psychotherapy: Theory Research and Practice*, **8**, 251–3.

Gaston, L. (1991) 'Reliability and criterion-related validity of the California Psychotherapy Alliance Sclaes-Patient version', *Psychological Assessment: A Journal of Consulting and Clinical Psychology*, **3**, 68–74.

Glasgow, D. and Eisenberg, N. (1987) *Current Issues in Clinical Psychology*. Avebury, Aldershot.

Goldberg, C. (1988) *On Being a Pyschotherapist: The Journey of the Healer*. New York, Gardner Press.

Goldberg, D. (1981) *General Health Questionnaire*. Windsor, NFER-Nelson Publishing Co.

Goldie, J. (1995) 'An outward bound experience as part of a counselling training course. An evaluation of the impact on individuals'. MEd Dissertation, University of Birmingham.

Grant, J. (1992) 'BAC accreditation – what value?', *Counselling*, **3**, 2.

Greenberg, R. P. and Staller, J. (1981) 'Personal therapy for therapists', *American Journal of Psychiatry*, **138**, 1467–71.

Greencavage, L. M. and Norcross, J. C. (1990) 'Where are the commonalities among the therapeutic common factors?', *Professional Psychology: Research and Practice*, **21**, 372–8.

Grimes, W. R. and Murdock, N. L. (1989) 'Social influence revisited: effects of counselor influence on outcome variables', *Psychotherapy*, **26**, 469–74.

Guy, J. D. (1987) *The Personal Life of a Psychotherapist*. Chichester, Wiley.

Guy, J. D. and Liaboe, G. P. (1986) 'The impact of conducting psychotherapy on psychotherapists' interpersonal functioning', *Professional Psychology: Research and Practice*, **17**, 111–14.

HMSO (1993) *Realising Our Potential: A Strategy for Science, Engineering and Technology*. London, HMSO.

Habeshaw, S., Gibbs, G. and Habeshaw, T. (1993) *53 Interesting Ways to Assess Your Students*. Melksham, Cromwell Press.

Hargie, O. D. W. (ed) (1986) *A Handbook of Communication Skills*. London, Routledge.

Hawkins, P. and Shohet, R. (1989) *Supervision in the Helping Profession*. Milton Keynes, Open University Press.

Henry, W. E., Sims, J. H. and Spray, S. L. (1971) *The Fifth Profession*. San Francisco, Jossey Bass.

Heppner, P. P. and Claiborn, C. D. (1989) 'Social influence research in counseling: a review and critique', *Journal of Counseling Psychology*, **36**, 365–87.

Heppner, P. P. and Peterson, C. H. (1982) 'The development and implications of a personal problem solving invention', *Journal of Counseling Psychology*, **29**, 66–75.

Hickox, M. (1995) 'Situating vocationalism', *British Journal of Sociology of Education*, **16**, 2, 153–63.

Higgins, R. L., Frisch, M. B. and Smith, D. (1983) 'A comparison of role play and natural responses to identical circumstances', *Behaviour Therapy*, **14**, 158–69.

Hoag, L. (1992) 'Psychotherapy in the general practice surgery: considerations of the frame', *British Journal of Psychotherapy*, **8**, 417–29.

Holt, R. R. and Luborsky, L. (1958) *Personality Patterns of Psychiatrists*. New York, Basic Books.

Hooper, D. (1995) *Individual Accreditation: Interim Report*. Rugby, British Association for Counselling.

Horton, I. (1995) 'Counsellor training courses: external roles and procedures', *Counselling*, **6**, 3, 183–4.

Horton, I. and Bayne, R. (1994) 'Some guidelines on the use of audio tape recordings in counsellor education and training', *Counselling*, **5**, 3, 213–4.

Howard, A. (1992) 'What, and why, are we accrediting?', *Counselling*, **3**, 2.

Ingram, R. E. and Zurawski, R. (1981) 'Choosing a clinical psychologist: an examination of the utilization of admissions criteria', *Professional Psychology*, **12**, 684–9.

Isis (1995) *Postgraduate Diploma in Counselling Practice: Course Document and Student Handbook*. Oxford, ISIS.

Ivey, A. E. (1971) *Microcounseling: Innovations in Interview Training*. Springfield, IL, Charles C. Thomas.

Ivey, A. E. and Authier, J. (1978) *Microcounseling: Innovations in Interviewing, Counseling, Psychotherapy and Psychoeducation* (2nd edition). Springfield, IL, Charles C. Thomas.

Izzard, S. A. and Wheeler, S. J. (1994) 'The development of self-awareness: an essential aspect of counsellor training? Does the provision of a personal awareness group as an integral part of counsellor training enhance the development of self-awareness?' *Paper to IRTAC conference, Munich, April.*

Jacobs, M. (1992) *Insight and Experience*. Buckingham, Open University Press.

Jessup, G. (1991) *Outcomes. NVQs and the Emerging Model of Education and Training.* London, Falmer.

Kagan, N., Kratewohl, D. and Miller, R. (1963) 'Stimulated recall in the therapy using videotape – a case study', *Journal of Counseling Psychology*, **10**, 237–43.

Kivlghan, D. M. and Quigley, S. T. (1991) 'Dimensions used by experienced and novice group therapists to conceptualise group process', *Journal of Counseling Psychology*, **38**, 4, 415–23.

Klein, R. H. and Babineau, R. (1974) 'Evaluating the competence of trainees: it's nothing personal', *American Journal of Psychiatry*, **131**, 7, 788–91.

LaCrosse, M. B. (1980) 'Perceived counselor influence and counseling outcomes', *Journal of Counseling Psychology*, **31**, 363–70.

Lafferrty, P., Beutler, L. E. and Crago, M. (1989) 'Differences between more and less effective psychotherapists: a study of select therapist variables', *Journal of Consulting and Clinical Psychology*, **57**, 76–80.

LaFramboise, T. D., Coleman, H. L. K. and Hernandez, A. (1991) 'Development and factor structure of the Cross Cultural Counseling Inventory–revised', *Professional Psychology, Research and Practice*, **22**, 380–8.

Lambert, M. J. and Bergin, A. E. (1983) 'Therapist characteristics and their contribution to psychotherapy outcome' in Walker, C. E. (ed) *The Handbook of Clinical Psychology*, **1**, 204–41. Homewood, IL, Dow Jones-Irwin.

Larson, L. M., Suzuki, L. A., Gillespie, K. N., Potenza, M. T., Bechtel, M. A. and Toulouse, A. L. (1992) 'Development and validation of the counseling self estimate inventory', *Journal of Counseling Psychology*, **39**, 1, 105–20.

Leong, F. T. L., Wagner, S. N. and Tata, S. P. (1995) 'Racial and ethnic variations in help-seeking atitudes' in Ponterotto, J. G., Casas, J. M., Suzuki, L. A. and Alexander, C. M. *Handbook of Multicultural Counseling*. London, Sage.

Levine, M. and Spivack, G. (1964) *The Rorschach Index of Repressive Style*. Springfield IL., Charles C. Thomas.

Liddle, B. J. (1995) 'Sexual orientation bias among graduate students of counseling and counseling psychology', *Counselor Education and Supervision*, **34**, 321–31.

Lietaer, G. (1992) 'Helping and hindering processes in client centred experiential psychotherapy: a content analysis of client and therapist post session perceptions' in Toukman-
ian, S. G. and Rennie, D. L. (eds) *Psychotherapy Process Research: Paradigmatic and
Narrative Approaches*. London, Sage, 134–62.

Linden, J. D., Stone, S. C. and Shertzer, B. (1965) 'Development and evaluation of an
inventory for rating counseling', *Personnel and Guidance Journal*, **44**, 267–76.

Liston, E. L., Yager, J. and Strauss, G. D. (1981) 'Assessment of psychotherapy skills: the
problem of Interrater Agreement', *American Journal of Psychiatry*, **138**, 8 August, 1069–
74.

Llewelyn, S. P., Elliot, R., Shapiro, D. A., Firth, J. and Hardy, G. (1987) 'Client perceptions
of significant events in prescriptive and exploratory phases of individual therapy', *British
Journal of Clinical Psychology*, **27**, 105–14.

Luborsky, L. (1976) 'Helping alliances in psychotherapy' in Claghorn, J. L. (ed) *Successful
Psychotherapy*. New York, Brunner/Mazel, 92–116.

Macaskill, N. D. (1988) 'Personal therapy in the training of the psychotherapist: is it
effective?', *British Journal of Psychotherapy*, **4**, 3, 219–26.

Macaskill, N. and Macaskill, A. (1992) 'Psychotherapists-in-training evaluate their personal
therapy: results of a UK survey', *British Journal of Psychotherapy*, **9**, 2, 133–8.

McConnaughy, E. A. (1987) 'The person of the therapist in psychotherapeutic practice',
Psychotherapy, **24**, 3, 303–14.

McLennan, J. (1994) 'The skills-based model of counsellor training: a review of the
evidence', *Australian Psychologist*, **29**, 2, 79–88.

McLeod, J. (1992) 'What do we know about how best to assess counsellor competence?',
Counselling Psychology Quarterly, **5**, 4, 359–72.

McLeod, J. (1993) *Introduction to Counselling*. Buckingham, Open University Press.

McLeod, J. (1994) *Doing Counselling Research*. London, Sage.

McLeod, J. (1995) 'The Stresses of Training Counsellors', Chapter 10 in Dryden, W. *The
Stresses of Counselling in Action*. London, Sage.

McLeod, J. (1996) 'Competence in Counselling' in Bayne, R., Horton, I. and Bimrose, J.
(eds) *New Directions on Counselling*. London, Routledge.

McLeod, J. and McLeod, J. (1993) 'The relationship between personal philosophy and
effectiveness in counsellors', *Counselling Psychology Quarterly*, **6**, 2, 121–9.

Manthei, R. J. (1980) 'The use of training groups in counsellor education', *New Zealand Counselling and Guidance Association Journal*, 3, 257–64.

Manthei, R. J. and Tuck, B. F. (1980) 'Effects of training on New Zealand school counsellors as measured by the Personal Orientation Inventory', *International Journal for the Advancement of Counselling*, 3, 257–64.

Marmar, C. R., Gaston, L., Gallagher, D. and Thompson, L. W. (1989) 'Toward the validation of the Californian Therapeutic Alliance Rating System', *Psychological Assessment*, 1, 46–52.

Martin, J. (1990) 'Confusions in psychological skills training', *Journal of Counseling and Development*, 68, 402–7.

Martin, J., Slemon, A. G., Heibert, B., Hallberg, E. T. and Cummins, A. L. (1989) 'Conceptualizations of novice and experienced counselors', *Journal of Counseling Psychology*, 36, 395–400.

Martin, T. (1992) 'Accreditation – the candidates perspective', *Counselling*, 3, 2.

Mintz, J. and Luborsky, L. (1971) 'Segments versus whole sessions: which is the best unit for psychotherapy process research?', *Journal of Abnormal Psychology*, 78, 180–91.

Moncher, F. J. and Prinz, R. J. (1991) 'Treatment fidelity in outcome studies', *Clinical Psychology Review*, 11, 247–66.

Mumford, E., Schlensinger, H., Cuerdon, T. and Scully, J. (1987) 'Ratings of videotaped simulated patient interviews and four other methods of evaluating psychiatry clerkship', *American Journal of Psychiatry*, 144, 316–22.

NCVQ (1995) *NVQ Criteria and Guidance*. London.

Nelson-Jones, R. and Patterson, C. H. (1975) 'Measuring client centred attitudes', *British Journal of Guidance and Counselling*, 3, 2, 228–36.

Networks (1994), newsletter of the Advice, Guidance, Counselling and Psychotherapy Lead Body, December, Welwyn, Herts.

Nevid, J. S. and Gildea, T. J. (1984) 'The admissions process in clinical training: the role of the personal interview', *Professional Psychology: Research and Practice*, 15, 1, 18–25.

Norcross, J. C. and Prochaska, J. O. (1986) 'Psychotherapist heal thyself: self-initiated and therapy-facilitated change of psychological distress', *Psychotherapy*, 23, 345–56.

O'Leary, E., Crowley, M. and Keane, N. (1994) 'A personal growth training group with trainee counsellors: outcome evaluation', *Counselling Psychology Quarterly*, 7, 2, 133–41.

Osgood, C. E., Suchi, G. T. and Tannenbaum, P. M. (1957) *The Measurement of Meaning.* Urbana, IL, University of Illinois Press.

Overholzer, J. C. (1993) 'Defining the boundaries of professional competence: managing subtle cases of clinical incompetence' in Mindell, J. A. (1993) *Issues in Clinical Psychology.* Duberque Inc., Wm C. Brown Communication Inc.

Page, R. C. and O'Leary, E. (1992) 'A pilot study of the effects of a training group on Irish counselling students', *Journal of Multicultural Counseling and Development*, **20**, 23–34.

Pates, A. and Knasel, E. (1989) 'Assessment of counselling skills development: the learning record', *British Journal of Guidance and Counselling*, **17**, 121–32.

Patterson, C. H. (1984) 'Empathy, warmth and genuineness in psychotherapy: a review of reviews', *Psychotherapy*, **21**, 431–8.

Pearce, A. (1994) 'Investigating biases in trainee counsellors' attitudes to clients from different cultures', *British Journal of Guidance and Counselling*, **22**, 3, 417–28.

Phillips, S. D. (1984) 'Contributions and limitations in the use of computers in counselor training', *Counselor Education and Supervision*, **24**, 2.

Ponterotto, J. G. and Furlong, M. J. (1985) 'Evaluating counselor effectiveness: a critical review of rating scale instruments', *Journal of Counseling Psychology*, **32**, 4, 597–616.

Ponterotto, J. G., Rieger, B. P., Barret, A. and Sparks, R. (1994) 'Assessing multicultural competence: a review of instrumentation', *Journal of Counseling and Development*, **72**, 316–22.

Ponterotto, J. G., Sanchez, C. M. and Magids, D. M. (1991) *Initial development and Validation of the Multicultural counseling awareness scale* (MCAS) (paper presented at the annual meeting of the American Pscyhological Association). San Francisco, CA.

Prochaska, J. O. and Norcross, J. C. (1983) 'Contemporary psychotherapists: a national survey of characteristics, practices, orientations and attitudes', *Psychotherapy: Theory Research and Practice*, **20**, 161–73.

Proctor, B. (1984) *Self Directed Learning: The South West London College Counselling Course. Self and Society* (whole issue).

Propst, I. R., Ostrom, R., Watkins, P., Dean, T. and Mashburn, D. (1992) 'Comparative efficacy of religious and non religious cognitive behavioural therapy for the treatment of clinical depression in religious individuals', *Journal of Consulting and Clinical Psychology*, **60**, 94–103.

Purton, C. (1991) 'Selection and assessment in counsellor training courses' in Dryden, W. and Thorne, B. *Training and Supervision for Counselling in Action*. London, Sage, 33–49.

Reik, T. (1948) *Listening With the Third Ear: The Inner Experience of a Psychoanalyst*. New York, Farrar and Strauss.

Ridgeway, I. R. (1990) 'Multiple measures for the prediction of counsellor trainee effectiveness', *Canadian Journal of Counselling*, **24**, 3, 165–77.

Robinson, W. L. (1974) 'Conscious competency, the mark of a competent instructor', *Personnel Journal*, **53**, 538–9.

Rogers, C. R. (1951) *Client Centred Therapy*. London, Constable.

Rogers, C. R. (1957) 'The necessary and sufficient conditions of therapeutic personality change', *Journal of Consulting Psychology*, **21**, 95–103.

Rogers, C. R. (1967) *On Becoming a Person: A Therapists View of Psychotherapy*. London, Constable.

Rosenberg, M. (1965) *Society and the Adolescent Self Image*. Princeton, New Jersey, Princeton University Press.

Roswell, V. A. (1993) 'Professional liability: issues for behaviour therapists in the 1980s and 1990s' in Mindell, J. A. *Issues in Clinical Psychology*. Dubuque, Wm C. Brown Communication Inc.

Rowe, W., Murphy, H. B. and De Csipkes, R. A. (1975) 'The relationship of counselor characteristics and counseling effectiveness', *Review of Educational Research*, **45**, 2, 231–46.

Rowntree, D. (1981) *Developing Courses for Students*. Maidenhead, McGraw-Hill.

RSA (1984) *Certificate in Counselling Skills in the Development of Learning: Notes for Guidance*. London, Royal Society of Arts.

Rudolph, J. (1988) 'Counselors' attitudes toward homosexuality: a selective review of the literature', *Journal of Counseling and Development*, **67**, 165–8.

Rushton, R. and Davis, H. (1992) 'An Evaluation of Training in Basic Counselling Skills', *British Journal of Guidance and Counselling*, **20**, 2, 205–20.

Russell, J. (1993) *Out of Bounds: Sexual Exploitation in Counselling and Therapy*. London, Sage.

Russell, J. and Dexter, G. (1993) 'Ménage à trois: accreditation, NVQs and BAC, *Counselling*, **4**, 4, 266–8.

Safinofsky, L. (1979) 'Evaluating the competence of psychotherapists', *Canadian Journal of Psychiatry*, **24**, 193–205.

Samuels, A. (1993) 'What is a good training?' *British Journal of Psychotherapy*, **9**, 3, 317–23.

Schon, D. (1987) *Educating the Reflective Practitioner*. London, Jossey Bass.

Scofield, M. E. and Yoxheimer, L. L. (1983) 'Psychometric issues in the assessment of clinical competencies', *Journal of Counseling Psychology*, **30**, 413–20.

Scott, P. (1995) *The Meanings of Mass Higher Education*. Milton Keynes, Open University Press.

Sexton, T. L. and Whiston, S. C. (1991) 'Review of the literature. A review of the empirical basis for counseling: implications for practice and training', *Counselor Education and Supervision*, **30**, 330–54.

Sharf, R. S. and Lucas, M. (1993) 'An assessment of a computerized simulation of counselling skills', *Counselor Education and Supervision*, **32**, 4, 254–66.

Sharpley, F. and Ridgeway, I. R. (1991) 'The relevance of previous knowledge on psychology to training in basic counselling skills', *British Journal of Guidance and Counselling*, **19**, 3, 299–306.

Sharpley, F. and Ridgeway, I. R. (1993) 'An evaluation of the effectiveness of Self efficacy as a predictor of trainee counselling skills performance', *British Journal of Guidance and Counseling*, **21**, 1, 73–81.

Sharpley, C. F., Guidara, D. A. and Rowley, M. A. (1994) 'Psychometric evaluation of a "standardized client" procedure with trainee counsellors', *Counselling Psychology Quarterly*, **7**, 1, 69–82.

Shaw, B. F. and Dobson, K. S. (1988) 'Competency judgements in the training and evaluation of psychotherapists', *Journal of Consulting and Clinical Psychology*, **56**, 5, 666–72.

Small, J. J. and Manthei, R. J. (1988) 'Group work in counsellor training: research and development in one programme', *British Journal of Guidance and Counselling*, **16**, 1, 33–49.

Sodowsky, G. R., Taffe, R. C., Gutkin, T. and Wise, S. L. (1995) 'Development and applications of the multicultural counseling inventory', *Journal of Counseling Psychology*.

Stevenson, J. F., Norcross, J. C., King, J. T. and Tobin, K. G. (1984) 'Evaluating clinical training programs: a formative effort', *Professional Psychology: Research and Practice*, **15**, 2, 218–29.

Stock-Whittaker, D. (1990) *Using Groups to Help People*. London, Routledge.

Stoltenberg, C. D. and Delworth, U. (1987) *Supervising Counselors and Therapists*. London, Jossey Bass.

Strong, S. R. (1968) 'Counseling: a social influence process', *Journal of Counseling Psychology*, **15**, 215–24.

Strong, S. R. and Dixon, D. N. (1971) 'Expertness, attractiveness and influence in counseling', *Journal of Counseling Psychology*, **18**, 562–70.

Strupp, H. H. (1959) 'Towards the analysis of the therapist's contribution to the treatment process', *Psychiatry*, **22**, 4, 349–62.

Strupp, H. H. and Binder, J. L. (1984) *Psychotherapy in a New Key: A Guide to Time Limited Dynamic Psychotherapy*. New York, Basic Books.

Strupp, H. H., Butler, S. and Rosser, C. (1988) 'Training in psychodynamic therapy, *Journal of Consulting and Clinical Psychology*, **56**, 5, 689–95.

Sue, D. W., Bernier, J. E., Durran, A., Feinberg, L., Pederson, P. B., Smith, E. J. and Vasquez-Nuttal, E. (1982) 'Position paper: cross cultural counseling competencies', *Counselling Psychologist*, **10**, 45–52.

Sue, D. W. and Sue, D. (1990) *Counselling the Culturally Different: Theory and Practice*. New York, Wiley.

Syme, G. (1995) *Counselling in Private Practice*. London, Routledge.

Thompson, H. and Vickers, K. (1995) *Diploma in Integrative Psychosynthesis Counselling: Course Handbook*. London, Communication and Counselling Foundation.

Truax, C. and Carkhuff, R. R. (1967) *Towards Effective Counselling and Psychotherapy: Training and Practice*. New York, Aldine.

The University of Birmingham (1995) Faculty Handbook, Faculty of Education and Continuing Studies.

Vacc, N. A. and Loesch, L. C. (1993) 'A content analysis of opinions about the National Counselor Examination', *Journal of Counseling and Development*, **71**, 4, 418–21.

Vickers, K. and Thompson, H. (1995) Brochure for the Diploma in Integrative Psychosynthesis Counselling, The Communication and Counselling Foundation.

Wagner, C. A. and Smith, J. P. (1979) 'Peer supervision: toward more effective training', *Counselor Education and Supervision*, **18**, 4.

Wheeler, S. (1991) 'Personal therapy: an essential aspect of counsellor training, or a distraction from focussing on the client?', *International Journal for the Advancement of Counselling*, **14**, 193–202.

Wheeler, S. (1993) 'Reservations about eclectic and integrative approaches to counselling' in Dryden, W. *Questions and Answers on Counselling in Action*. London, Sage.

Wheeler, S. (1994) 'Choosing a course: all that glitters is not gold', *Counselling*, **5**, 3, 210–12.

Wheeler, S. (1996) 'Counselling a dying client: Confrontation or compassion, counter-transference or collusion?', *Psychodynamic Counselling*, **2**, 2, (in press).

White, G. D. and Pollard, J. (1982) 'Assessing therapeutic competence from therapy session attendance', *Professional Psycholgoy*, **13**, 5, 628–31.

White, P. E. and Franzoni, J. (1990) 'A multidimensional analysis of the mental health of graduate counselors in training', *Counselor Education and Supervision*, **29**, 259–67.

Whiteley, J. M., Sprinthall, N. A., Mosher, R. L. and Donaghy, R. T. (1967) 'Selection and evaluation of counselor effectiveness', *Journal of Counseling Psychology*, **14**, 226–34.

Whitely, J. (1969) 'Counselor education', *Review of Educational Research*, **39**, 173–89.

Wiley, M. O. and Ray, P. B. (1986) 'Counseling Supervision by Developmental Level', *Journal of Counseling Psychology*, **33**, 439–45.

Williams, K. E. and Chambless, P. L. (1990) 'The relationship between the characteristics and outcome of in vivo explosive treatment for agoraphobia', *Behaviour Therapy*, **21**, 111–16.

Wogan, M. (1970) 'Effect of therapist patient personality variables on therapeutic outcome', *Journal of Consulting and Clinical Psychology*, **35**, 356–61.

Wolf, A. (1995) *Competence-based Assessment*. Buckingham, Open University Press.

Woolfe, R. (1983) 'Counselling in a world of crisis: toward a sociology of counselling', *International Journal for the Advancement of Counselling*, **6**, 167–76.

Index